Flea Market
Fabulous

Flea Market

Fabulous

DESIGNING GORGEOUS ROOMS
WITH VINTAGE TREASURES

LARA SPENCER

WITH AMY FEEZOR

Foreword by Jonathan Adler

Photographs by ChiChi Ubiña

STEWART, TABORI & CHANG NEW YORK

MICHAËL BORREMANS – THE PERFORMANCE

Gordon Matta-Clark
Works and Collected Writings
Gloria Moure

20_21 Collection   Ediciones Poligrafa

Francis Alÿs · Cuauhtémoc Medina   WHEN FAITH MOVES MOUNTAINS
                                    CUANDO LA FE MUEVE MONTAÑAS

Files

Stuff

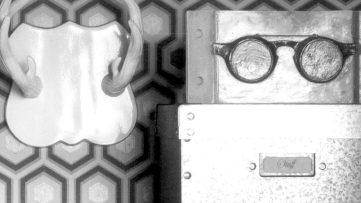

33rd Punjabis
1915

INDIA

Table of Contents

FOREWORD

Jonny decorated my GMA dressing room in the most glorious explosion of color EVER! It's impossible not to be in a good mood in there—even at 4a.m.!

First off, let me say that Lara should probably not read this foreword. I am about to blow a major amount of hot air up her skirt and I would not want her to read it and then become all conceited and horrid. I would not want her to change.

I love Lara because Lara is fab, Lara is fun, and Lara is a very **groovy gal**. The truth is that Lara can light up a room. When Lara arrives the party gets started. Her contagious humor and wicked spontaneity infiltrate every nook and cranny. She is a **tornado of blonde positivity**. That chick has charisma.

But here's the deal: not only can she light up a room metaphorically—changing the mood from **greige to kapow**—but she can do it literally, too. Lara's creativity and her design genius are every bit as powerful as her personal charisma. She has the magical ability to walk into a room and transform the vibe from **soggy to glam** . . . all without spending a billion dollars. She makes chic affordable and accessible!

In this book you get to accompany Lara as she shines her **love-light** on nine very different design challenges. You can follow her to the flea market and the upholsterer. You get to slosh paint with her and swag a drape or two.

This is a very generous book. Lara did not phone it in. **Au contraire!** She has slaved her guts out to bring you a cavalcade of creative solutions and a fiesta of panache-riddled flourishes. Most importantly, Lara is on a mission to help you, dear reader, to make your home fabulous and thereby add **fabulosity** to your life. Lara has a missionary zeal to bring glamour and color to your home and glamour and color to your life.

Let me sum it up for you: Lara is **life-enhancing**. I would needlepoint this phrase on a pillow, but I would not want her to read it and then get a big head.

Jonathan Adler

Potter and committed Lara-phile

"Lara lights up the world!"

introduction

Hello again, fellow flea market fanatics, yard sale junkies, and thrift shop connoisseurs! As some of you might know, in my first book, I Brake For Yard Sales, I shared all of the treasure hunting tips my mom, the ultimate yard saler, taught me. In Flea Market Fabulous, I put all of that know-how to work using all of my secondhand scores to create spaces that only look like they cost a million bucks! In the following pages, we'll be decorating nine very different rooms using almost entirely all rescued, recycled, and reinvented pieces found at our usual haunts—thrift shops, yard sales, and flea markets—including the mecca for vintage treasures: the Brimfield Antique Show in Brimfield, Massachusetts.

Robin and I talk design during commercial breaks on the set of *Good Morning America*.

ABOVE I spy with my little eye . . . a nineteenth-century telescope at Elephant's Trunk Flea Market in New Milford, Connecticut. It's open every Sunday from March through the beginning of December.

LEFT Cameras roll as we shop for an HGTV special called *I Brake for Yard Sales*. By the way, I didn't buy that $75 painting and still regret it!

From Reel Life to Real Life

HGTV asked me to do a series based on my first book, *I Brake for Yard Sales*, in which viewers can watch my team and me solve real-life design dilemmas using all of our secondhand scores and rehab know-how . . .

In this book you'll see real rooms belonging to families with real design dilemmas. There's the couple so terrified of making a mistake while decorating their living room that they just let it sit empty—for *four* years! There's another couple who wanted to turn their dark and dismal basement into a fun playroom for their little boy, and a place they could entertain grown-up friends as well. Let me tell you, it was daunting, but also incredibly gratifying, to turn a cavernous unused space into a beautiful room that hardly resembles the basement it once was. If that dilemma sounds familiar—whether it's your basement or attic or a quirky little room you have no idea what to do with—I promise, you will find an idea in the makeovers you're about to see.

There is inspiration everywhere in this book regardless of your design dilemma. One of my favorite challenges is a kitchen belonging to a couple who never got around to decorating because the wife was diagnosed with

BELOW Members of "the team"—Jen, Cija, and Alex—watch a video of one of the design dilemmas with me and brainstorm how we'll solve it.

ABOVE Behind the scenes in the oh-so-glamorous world of an HGTV makeover. Hey, safety before beauty. Always.

breast cancer right after they moved in (chapter 8). Now in remission, she is ready to celebrate with food, friends, and a fashionable kitchen that captures the essence of her spirit and zest for life. She felt she was given a second chance, and loved the idea of a room filled with pieces that were as well.

So, what's your style? It's okay if you don't know. I bet you'll figure it out by the time you get to the end of this book. Not that it will be set in stone. Mine has changed a dozen times over the years. The rooms I loved when I was younger were always more serious—filled with plaids and lots of brown antiques. Now I feel no need to prove I have a "grown-up" home. My style is much more who I really am—quirky and eclectic—a mix of sleek mid-century pieces with comfortable, relaxed seating, and art that makes me smile.

And that's why flea markets are indeed *fabulous*! They are filled with magical and mysterious objects that are just screaming to be brought into our homes to create rooms that make us happy.

Whether or not they are true diamonds in the rough—bought for a song, and actually worth a fortune—doesn't really matter. I mean, don't get me wrong. I will never forget the antique prints I bought for ten dollars that were actually worth ten thousand—but that doesn't happen often, so don't race off to a flea market just yet. What *really* matters is what your flea market finds mean to you—and how they make you feel. The rooms I love the most are the ones that tell a story. *Your* story.

Sam & I goofing off at her upholstery shop, Tiger Lily's!

The A Team

There is no group I would rather get down and dirty with than The Spectacular Six—my television design team who are all experts in different areas of home design. In this book, you will see their handiwork in wood restoration, custom furniture building, electrical, upholstery, and decorative painting. Trust me, this group has it covered like nobody's business and they'll share their knowledge with you throughout this book.

Alex Guerrero

AWESOME AT

Painting, refinishing, and reinventing furniture. Also awesome at making you smile at the end of a long day.

STYLE AT HOME

My style is a bit eclectic and DIY. I've got art to the ceilings—even resting on top of molding on the doors. Every west-facing window is flush with plants and a crystal chandelier refracts afternoon light.

FAVORITE FLEA FIND

A beautiful 1930s brass and cast-iron wood stove that had been sitting in a barn forever. Alas, I rent, so I had to walk away from it.

Cija Johnson

AWESOME AT

Specialty painting (faux finishing, color matching, etc.), finish carpentry, and problem solving. Also makes a mean lasagna and speaks Italian . . . sort of.

STYLE AT HOME

I call my style "Hollywood Flea-gency." I love the Hollywood Regency look, with hints of vintage flea market finds blended in.

FAVORITE FLEA FIND

A pristine 1920s German blue marbled glass light shade I got from Brimfield for $120. It's perfect in our condo, which is of the same era!

David Dall

AWESOME AT

Engineering and fabrication of large and small mechanical creations, electrical lighting, and custom home building. Also awesome at offshore powerboat racing, being Super Dad, and wearing mismatched socks.

STYLE AT HOME

The new kitchen that I'm building in my house has contemporary cabinets with 200-year-old hand-hewn beams running across the ceiling and vintage tin tobacco press panels for backsplashes.

FAVORITE FLEA FIND

Seven hand-sketched nudes for $25 that turned out to be signed original drawings by Henri Matisse!

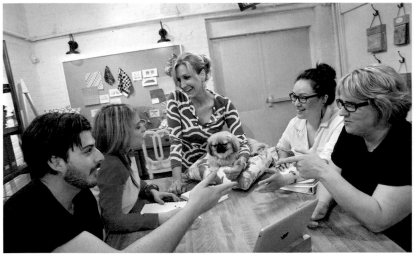

Jen Chu

AWESOME AT

Project management, design layout, and decorative painting. Also awesome at playing pop songs by ear on the piano.

STYLE AT HOME

My style these days can be described as "Nate Berkus globe-trots on a budget." Neutral palette, contemporary but warm, slightly masculine, with Buddha figurines and Colombian masks.

FAVORITE FLEA FIND

A 1940s cast brass chandelier from Brooklyn Flea for $125. I also scored an amazing nineteenth-century French armchair left by someone on trash day. I had it repaired and reupholstered and absolutely love it!

Mark Devito

AWESOME AT

Furniture repair, transformation, and restoration. Also awesome at playing bass guitar and making silly short movies.

STYLE AT HOME

My house is colonial style and I like nineteenth-century American furniture and reproductions made by my dad. Those pieces are treasures to me.

FAVORITE FLEA FIND

A dirty, chipped antique gold-leaf mirror for $100. Pressed between its backboard and mirror, I found a poster from a French perfume company that dated back to 1810. The colors were absolutely beautiful; it was in perfect condition.

Sam Knapp

AWESOME AT

Fabric selection, upholstery redesign, and window treatment concepts. Also awesome at taking photos of the great outdoors.

STYLE AT HOME

Style for me is personal self-expression. I am always looking to push my own boundaries, which creates a dynamic end result. It is never the same twice.

FAVORITE FLEA FIND

Vintage French elk-horn sconces with the bulbs encased in beads and crystals. I found them right after I moved from the Upper East Side to a Connecticut cottage, so the look was perfect—fancy girl meets rustic country lifestyle.

The Countdown: 48 Hours

If you think decorating a room is stressful—try doing it in just 48 hours on a tiny budget, and in front of cameras!

Wallpaper going up, stripes going down!

David and I making emergency carpet repairs.

All Hands on Deck

All of our flea market finds were transformed back at our workshop then set aside until "The Installation"—two days when a family would move out and we would take over. The first day, we'd clear the room, and then, depending on the project, wallpaper, paint, rip apart, or build. On day two, we installed furniture right down to the tiniest accessories—all in time to surprise the family (with cameras rolling, of course) by the day's end. We worked at breakneck speed, but with my team of experts, we were able to accomplish incredible things. Not that there wasn't a snafu or two along the way. Each subsequent room makeover got easier—we got better at time management and remembered the golden rule of decorating: HAVE FUN. It's not the end of the world if something breaks or doesn't fit like you think it will. You know the old saying, "There's a million ways to skin a cat"? Well, there are plenty of ways to decorate a room—and the fun is discovering which way you like best.

ABOVE I guess David was tired of me talking while he raced to finish the project. Needless to say, I got the hint!

ABOVE Jen on her tiptoes helping Alex install a canopy bed.

LEFT Fingers crossed! The camera captures me looking more than a little nervous as I wait for the family to walk into their new media room.

The homeowners see their crisp new kitchen for the first time!

A Moment Like This

Showing the homeowners their redone rooms for the first time was an amazingly gratifying moment for us. We listened to their dilemmas, and asked them a zillion questions about what they wanted and didn't want. We searched their homes for clues to their style and favorite colors, and we asked them to show us pictures of things that appealed to them. We used all that information to create rooms they would love—but at the end of the day, we still held our breath and prayed they were as happy with the redone rooms as we were. I am thrilled to say, we were nine for nine (yes, I'm including me as one of the homeowners). Doing the research really paid off. Whether you're decorating yourself or having someone do it for you, be sure to start a file or make a design board like the ones you'll see in this book. They'll help ensure your "big reveal" is a great one.

chapter 1

A LIVELY LIVING ROOM

The first time I walked into this home, I was greeted by three energetic little girls who stormed though their big empty living room like it was a racetrack. For years, the homeowners tolerated empty white walls, bare wood floors, and hardly a stick of furniture. They were finally ready to break away from boring beige, but had serious color commitment issues—too many options overwhelmed them, and they were so worried they'd make a mistake they were paralyzed. Decorating this room had proved daunting, so they asked me to help them take the plunge.

1

THE ROOM HAS
NO PERSONALITY.

2

THE COUPLE
WANTS COLOR
BUT THEY ARE
TERRIFIED OF IT.

3

THE SPACE IS
LARGE AND
NARROW, AND
LACKS WARMTH
AND COZINESS.

The Plan

Bringing life to a "non"-living room

When I did a little investigating around this house, I saw bits of blue and hints of ravishing red. As for patterned fabric, the couple claimed to "hate them all" and yet I spotted accents of ikat and toile in their other rooms. They did have a style, they just didn't realize it yet. I met with the team, made a shopping list, and came up with a game plan.

On my to-do list:

- Give the couple the color they desire but were still skittish about. We will leave the walls white and go crazy with color in places that aren't as big of a commitment—window treatments, pillows, and other accessories.

- Since the home already has a family room, we will make this a sophisticated space tailored for grown-ups.

- Make the vast room feel cozier and come up with a floor plan that offers a central seating area in front of the beautiful fireplace.

- Reinvent the pair of plaid bergère chairs (a fancy word for upholstered armchairs) that were a family heirloom.

We'll reuse these chairs, but they'll need a major update!

The only decor in this living room? A pair of outdated chairs, an overstuffed '80s sofa from the wife's single days, and two folding chairs . . . for when company comes over. Not exactly warm and cozy.

INSPIRATIONS

– shopping list –

- A great sofa—to complement the existing chairs

- Extra seating for entertaining

- A coffee table

- Several tables and chests—to provide storage and places to put lamps (there's no overhead lighting)

- Pairs of lamps

- A desk—the homeowners have requested a place to pay bills and write thank-you notes

- Art, accessories, and fabrics to add pops of color

The Hunt

All I have to work with so far is one pair of frumpy chairs, so I will need to start from scratch. I'm searching for big furniture, small accessories, and everything in between.

This English-style chest has clean lines, a classic shape, and was only $20 at an estate sale.

RIGHT African textiles like this one I found at the Antiques Garage in New York City make great pillows or throw blankets.

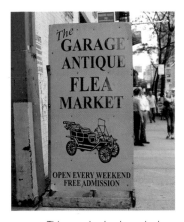

BELOW This stunning bookcase had my name written all over it. The faux-bamboo frame and slender proportions are perfect for between the room's windows.

SHOPPING FROM SCRATCH

To bring this empty living room to life, I knew I'd be plenty busy at flea markets and estate sales. Here are some of my tricks for shopping from scratch.

1. Understand the needs and function of your space.

2. Have a clear idea of what you want the room to look like. Bring tear sheets from design magazines (or my book) to inspire you.

3. Scale is key. A coffee table needs to agree with the sofa. Club chairs can't look too dinky or too overpowering. Side tables shouldn't be taller than the seating (but also shouldn't be too short).

4. Take measurements of all your pieces on a notepad or your smartphone so you have them on hand. You never know when a shopportunity might arise!

5. Do your homework, and budget accordingly. The most costly items will be upholstery, custom painting, and window treatments.

the big REVEAL

THIS LIVING ROOM has gone from boring to bold. With one-of-a-kind finds and some secondhand know-how, it has been transformed into a space that feels young, yet cultivated over time. The best part? The whole thing was led by the homeowners' own style, which we discovered in colors and pieces they used in other parts of the house. The room's white walls are the ideal backdrop for pops of navy blue and coral-infused red. Layers of pattern add texture and warmth to the space, which is now a living room worth living in!

before

$50

before

Fabric guru Sam used a leftover piece of fabric—also known as a remnant—to transform these flea market stools.

Going for Good Bones

If you read my first book, *I Brake for Yard Sales*, you already have my main rule ingrained in your brain. Repeat after me: When seeking out secondhand pieces, go for "good bones." Solid construction, iconic shapes, and great details will act as the foundation for a new, updated look. Custom upholstery or a new paint finish will transform your finds into something that's truly one of a kind.

For this family, I needed a sofa that was substantial enough to stand up to their large bergère chairs, yet not so big that it overwhelmed the room. I knew right away a green corduroy sofa I found for $50 was the perfect companion for the more ornate Frenchies. While the olive green fabric was faded and tired, you couldn't hide the mid-century sleekness of the arms, referred to as "Larsen style." The sofa was reupholstered in a red linen with a welt in soft blue to tie in the colors of the space. At the end of the day, I spent $800, but a similar sofa would cost three to four times as much in a retail shop.

New upholstery accentuates the elegant curves on this formerly tragic bench.

$20

LEFT AND ABOVE I called this "The Tragedy Bench" when I bought it because it was a mess—but had such great potential! With carved ball and claw feet and a unique size and shape, it was more than worth its $20 price tag. Two yards of toile fabric turned the beast into a real beauty.

"Before placing an order for fabric, be sure to ask for a sample to confirm its true color and quality."

—SAM

1. I literally scaled mountains of vintage furniture at Black Rock Galleries to unearth this. It's the back of a bench that had come apart, but I had another idea for the $50 find.

This carved wood panel is the perfect size for a console table!

2. Nice legs! I'll remove them from this $18 table and use them to turn the bench back into a table.

3. We built a frame to attach the legs then painted them to match the top. Total cost: $68!

I'm always on the lookout for great pairs of stools like these because they nestle nicely under any console or desk and are great as extra seating for company!

before

All Together Now

Many people have a tendency to line furniture along a room's walls to give the illusion of spaciousness. Unfortunately, that creates awkward conversation areas and results in a lot of wasted space. Instead, I prefer moving furniture off the walls, allowing it to float in the middle of a room. It's a much more social layout and brings attention to the focal point of the room: the elegant fireplace.

The console table we made using flea market finds (see left) not only hides the back side of the sofa, but also provides a place to put much-needed lighting. The black metal lamps were found at an estate sale for $20 each and dynamic stools under the table add sophisticated symmetry to the space.

$68

$35

The coral colored fabric draws your eye to the accessories in the bookcase!

before

$20

ABOVE To line the inside of the hutch, we simply cut fabric to size and used spray adhesive to attach it. A tiny print is ideal because you don't have to line the pattern up perfectly.

An Inside Job

I snatched up this hutch the minute I saw it. Even in a huge secondhand emporium like Black Rock Galleries, it's rare to find a piece this size that is sleek and unfussy—especially one that has great details like brass ring pulls, shield-shape keyholes, and the original keys! Its grand proportions balanced out the fireplace at the opposite end of the room, and it also added ample storage and the illusion of higher ceilings. The interior of the hutch was another matter. It had been covered in leopard contact paper that was peeling and not exactly in keeping with the family's style. Once we removed it, we lined the interior with a coral print fabric, which keeps the big black hutch from looking too stuffy. You can also use wallpaper or paint to add a contrasting pop of color to a bookcase or built-in shelves.

$60

A Star Is Born

Can't afford to buy an entire collection of original art? Make your own! We removed the glass from store-bought frames, then lined the back with scraps of grass-cloth wallpaper. The starfish was then glued to the center of each frame and for less than $75, we had created unique and interesting heirlooms. You can also do this with shells, vintage keys, or any lightweight trinkets. Make a statement by hanging several in a gallery-like grouping.

"Art doesn't have to be behind glass in a frame. Think outside the box and wall-mount your flea market finds."

—CIJA

RIGHT This basket was originally used for harvesting grapes. When I saw it, I immediately envisioned it as a dramatic piece of wall art. To break up the brown, we wired a flea-found brass tray from Argentina to the center of the piece.

Double Duty

We gave many pieces in this room new life and purpose—like this set of three nesting tables. We used just the tops, which were beautifully hand-painted, as frames for a trio of one-of-a-kind wall mirrors. See the opposite page for the end result.

before

1. Wobbly and beat up, these legs needed to be amputated—stat. But the tops were worth saving. They were beautifully painted with an Asian motif and will live on as wall art!

2. We detached the legs as well as the clear glass inserts— a simple task with a screwdriver.

3. Meanwhile, I had a local glass store cut three mirrors the same sizes as the glass tops.

4. The team and I inserted the new mirrors into the frames, then touched up the black edges with a permanent marker.

before

French Twist

These bergère chairs were well made, but their plaid fabric and gold finish had seen better days. We gave the wood frame a quick whitewash and reupholstered them using a large-scale fern print. The organic motif is a nice contrast to the stronger patterns and colors in the room, and the homeowners are thrilled we recycled a family heirloom.

These were the
nesting tables on
the opposite page!

$75

$250

$35

$40

All of these pieces came from thrift shops and cost less than $10 apiece!

ABOVE This vintage wood-carved mirror with a Greek key design is the perfect size for the space over the fireplace. Dating back to the '50s or '60s, it was a fabulous find at just $40.

FAR LEFT AND LEFT Jen and I used black acrylic paint to highlight the Asian motif used in the four corners of the mirror.

When arranging accessories, there is no real right or wrong—so just experiment! I like to make sure the heights are varied while keeping the overall scale balanced.

$35

Power in Numbers

To make it seem like the family had amassed collections over the years, I looked for objects that could be grouped by a common theme. While shopping for this room, one of those themes found me: blue and white Asian-influenced urns and vases that seemed to pop up at every flea market. The abundance—and their affordable price tag—made it a cinch to create a collection that looked like it was handed down or collected over the years. In truth? They all came from thrift shops or flea markets and most were under $10!

Rather than spreading them individually around the room, I flanked the mirror on the mantle with two clusters for maximum impact. My styling secret? As I arrange, I take pictures with my smartphone to see if anything looks funny or imbalanced and just keep playing with the layout until it feels right.

"Antique sconces can cost hundreds or even thousands of dollars. Why not look for pairs of things that can be wired for a fraction of the price?"

—DAVID

David and I transform the oil lamps—once used on a horse-drawn carriage—into electrified sconces. All the parts needed can be purchased at a hardware store for under $20!

$15

$8

$1

Brass Is Back

It's been the ugly stepchild of metal finishes for years, but more and more designers are turning back to brass for its timeless elegance and warm glow. The best news? You can find myriad brass and bronze-tone accessories at flea markets and thrift shops for next to nothing.

ABOVE Mix your metals! Brass and chrome work together beautifully on these '60s lamps with bamboo detailing.

RIGHT A brass cigarette holder shaped like a globe only cost $11!

A Final Thought

This was the first of eight rooms we redid for the *I Brake for Yard Sales* specials for HGTV, so it's near and dear to my heart—but it also nearly gave me a heart attack! It was the first time I've installed an entire room in ONE day, and of course, there were some unexpected fiascoes. The glass top for the coffee table broke and I sliced my finger on it. The curtains we made were two inches too short and looked like dorky high-water pants. Thankfully, Sam included a big hem so we were able to let them out for the extra length we needed. (A hem is always a good idea for this very reason.) In the end, we got another piece of glass cut in the nick of time, the curtains looked fab, and the family had no idea that creating their laid-back living room was anything but!

A piece of fabric became my "designer" band-aid.

We had to get creative when I cut my finger on broken glass.

chapter 2

A BEAUTIFUL BEDROOM

These newlyweds are living in the house he grew up in—and spending their first nights as husband and wife in his parents' old bedroom. We're talking the same bed, same dresser, even the exact same layout as it was when he was a little boy. Needless to say, that doesn't exactly work for the new missus. He, on the other hand, feels that it's perfectly fine and doesn't see a problem with it, but she'd like to start fresh and create a modern yet romantic love nest. I believe they will both fall in love with the end result of our work— because in design, as in love, compromise doesn't have to mean concession.

1

THE ROOM IS
STUCK IN A MID-
'70s TIME WARP.

2

IT'S HARD TO FEEL
SEXY IN YOUR IN-
LAWS' BED!

3

ASYMMETRICAL
WINDOWS AND
FOUR DOORWAYS
LIMIT LAYOUT
OPTIONS.

The Plan

Transforming things from "theirs" to "ours"

All the furniture in what had been his parents' bedroom was perfectly functional, but it had a brown, 1970s faux-colonial look—hardly conjuring up images of newly-wedded bliss! As huge believers in recycling, we'll repurpose almost everything. With the help of new paint and pulls. We'll reinvent the four-poster bed so it serves as a sexy centerpiece in the room while giving it the appearance of higher ceilings. The husband also says he would be willing to shake up the color palette as long as it was "nautical." His wife loves the ocean as well, so there is some common ground we can start with as a jumping-off point.

On my to-do list:

- Repaint the couple's existing furniture and change out the dated hardware.

- Add soft colors, texture, and visual interest to distract from low ceiling and odd-shaped room.

- Add a seating area so the room becomes a place to lounge and relax.

The starting point in this room is the ikat rug, which the wife had recently purchased. Its soft ocean colors will inspire our soothing, sexy palette.

The TV is moving to the family room to make space for a loungy seating area.

INSPIRATIONS

RIGHT These '60s glazed ceramic lamps were hiding in plain sight at a flea market. They were in perfect condition and a great color for the bedroom.

BELOW I loved this driftwood mirror I found at a flea market. Not only does it work with the seaside vibe I'm going for, but it's also a great piece of one-of-a-kind art. It's like nature's version of every decorator's favorite: the sunburst mirror.

The Hunt

I have to balance the bride's request for change with the groom's childhood ties to the room. I also want to find pieces that are serene and sexy.

YOU BREAK IT, YOU BUY IT (AND OTHER FLEA MARKET RULES)

Keep these in mind when shopping secondhand:

1. It's an unspoken law at flea markets—if you break something, you are expected to buy it. Dealers rely on people to be honest and understand that the margins on their one-of-a-kind finds aren't big, so this is one rule that should always be respected.

2. Early bird gets the worm. Pay the early shopping entrance fee—it's often just a few dollars and gives you a first crack at the good stuff.

3. Wear layers. It's usually cold in the early morning and steamy by the afternoon. Don't forget to throw some sunblock and a hat in your bag!

4. Bring your smartphone to research your potential treasures.

5. Bring a list of what you're looking for to stay focused. Also write down the measurements of any artwork you need framed. Flea markets have loads of cool old frames for next to nothing!

-shopping list-

- Cozy chairs to create a separate seating area

- Storage (she needs more drawer space)

- Table lamps to create sexier lighting

- Beachy artwork and accessories

- Something special for her—to make it feel like this is truly her room, too

Vintage maps make great art!

RIGHT Crafted on the island of Murano outside Venice, Italy, Murano glass is hand-blown using age-old techniques. It is richly colored and patterned, often sensuously shaped— and normally very expensive. Imagine my surprise when I spotted this tall, curvy lamp for $150 at a flea market! That's a fraction of what it would cost in a retail shop!

ABOVE This pair of '40s-style bucket chairs were practically a giveaway at an estate sale for $40, and it's easy to see why. Beneath the old, cat-clawed fabric, though, was a pair of fantastic club chairs just waiting to be recovered.

TOP The soft colors in this map are exactly what I had in mind for our nautical room.

the big REVEAL

CAN YOU GUESS HOW MANY PIECES we were able to recycle from the husband's parents' bedroom? All but one! In the end, we were able to use four of the room's five existing pieces, but looking at this space, you would never know they were the same ones. With a little ingenuity and some serious elbow grease, we were able to rescue, recycle, and reinvent them to create a room they both love—and where the honeymoon hopefully never ends.

before

$20

$30

$10

"Don't be afraid to paint a wood floor. A quality porch paint will hold up well, even with everyday wear and tear."

Earning Our Stripes

before

The hardwood floors were in great shape, but the color wasn't right. Instead of stripping and re-staining them, we chose to create a beachy look by painting 12-inch awning stripes using patio and floor paint in soft blue and creamy white.

To get the look, we first lightly sanded the floors. After a thorough wipe down, we painted the entire floor white and gave it a full day to dry. The next morning we measured out our stripes and used painter's tape to ensure clean lines. The colors are Grand Teton White and Seacliff Heights by Benjamin Moore, and two coats of each were all it took to achieve a flawless finish.

RIGHT Stripes generally look better running horizontally. (In other words, running along the wider dimension of the room.) It makes the space look more expansive.

RIGHT When you're painting a floor, it's important to keep the environment dust free. We took off our shoes, made sure to start from the inside corner, and gradually painted ourselves out of the room!

ABOVE The fabric on these pillows matches the room's color scheme. Ocean-inspired hues give the soft look she desires and meets the husband's request for a nautical vibe.

before

BUILDING UP A BREATHTAKING BED

The four-poster bed gets a dramatic canopy that makes it a cozy cocoon. Here's how we did it.

- The couple's bed wasn't tall enough to accommodate a canopy, so we added 18 inches of height by attaching lightweight aluminum poles to the four posts.

- The entire bed was painted shiny white to hide our handiwork.

- We also used pipe to build a rectangular frame overhead.

- We hung pleated curtains along the head of the bed first, then pulled the custom canopy up and over the support structure.

- The fabric was pulled taut and secured with staples.

ABOVE The couple's nightstands look fresh in apple green paint, and the flea market lamps are the perfect height for reading.

RIGHT Maps of coastal areas evoke the sea without being hokey or cliché. A single map is fine, but a group of maps makes a statement. Think about the places you've been or dream to go and search for them on your next flea market adventure.

"Canopies add instant romance to a bedroom. You can have them custom made, or you can drape store-bought curtains for a similar effect."

—SAM

This lamp is sitting on a midcentury table bought for just $10!

$20

Don't be scared away by stuff like this. Look how great it can become!

before

I knew they had great potential, but when Sam took the fabric off the "cat chairs," we realized they were also very well made.

The Cat's Meow

Don't judge a book by its cover—or a chair by its cat-clawed fabric. When Sam and the team stripped these $20 chairs for reupholstery, they discovered the construction of the mid-century barrel-backs was of the highest quality and well worth saving. Now that they're reupholstered in a luxurious fabric, you can see their great bones and classic shape. Covered in a fresh turquoise and white print, these would easily be priced at over a thousand dollars at a retail design shop.

The Sunny Side

The face on this $16 mid-century clock was broken, but the carved wooden sunburst around it was a star. After removing the clock mechanism, we glued a small round mirror in its place—an easy fix and terrific update!

Popping out the clock was super simple with a screw driver.

$16

$5 foo dog!

$75

This tall, narrow chest gives the wife the storage she needs without taking up much space. Painted in apple green and paired with the sunburst mirror, it's just the beam of sunshine this room needed!

Vanity Flair

The little mail table made of bamboo was chosen for its size and shape—definitely not its condition! Found at a flea market for just $30, it became a pretty vanity after we sanded off the chipped paint, then primed and painted it shiny white. Accessorized with a vintage silver tray and other feminine details, it is now a spot in the room that's just for the wife.

LEFT The scale of this estate-sale stool was perfect for our makeshift vanity (and was in excellent condition). To customize it for the bedroom's color scheme, we painted apple-green accents. It's the little details that can make a big impact!

Bedside Manner

The room's existing nightstands were boring, but they were the perfect size. Since there were so many soft and soothing colors in the room, we painted them a bright apple green to add some energy to the space. We replaced the hardware with shiny chrome boat cleats, a traditional nautical design used to secure ropes in place.

before

We bought these "drawer pulls" at a marine supply store!

We chose this textured wallpaper because it's the color of beach glass!

RIGHT Roman shades are more casual than curtains, and less expensive to make because they use less fabric. Since the windows are small, we went for a big impact with the print—and lined them with blackout fabric to block the morning light.

before

Happy Together

Creating romance in a space doesn't mean filling it with red roses and stacking Jane Austen novels by the bed. It's about finding ways to be together, relax, reconnect, and escape the world for a while. That's why we included a separate seating area where the couple can spend time reading the Sunday paper or share a morning coffee. We had a limited amount of space, so we made sure the size and scale of each piece worked precisely.

Pretty & Paisley

Tables like the one below were popular in the eighteenth and nineteenth centuries because they were just the right size for a candle and a book. This one was missing its original leather top, but for only $80 at a furniture consignment shop, it was worth it. After a light sanding and a rubdown with wood wax, we used a scrap piece of the wallpaper to replace the leather insert on top, which tied it into the rest of the room.

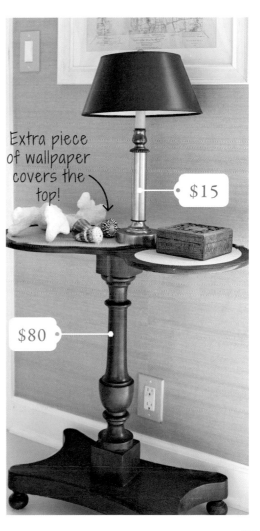

Extra piece of wallpaper covers the top!

$15

$80

before

"Wood wax is great for revitalizing older wood furniture. It brings out the color and takes only minutes to apply."

—DAVID

My butt did that!

before

ABOVE I followed Mark's advice when I found this old bench at Brimfield, and look what happened! Luckily it was an easy fix.

Breakthrough Moments

I fell in love with this ornate wicker bench i found at Brimfield, and the second I sat down, I found out the hard way the Victorian beauty wasn't quite as solid as she looked. When I busted through the seat, I knew had to buy it. (Remember: At a flea market, you break it, you buy it!) But that was just fine. With its warm patina and delicate curves, it was perfect for the end of the bed.

Repairing the wicker seat would have cost a fortune. Instead, we cut a piece of plywood to sit in its place, added a piece of foam, and covered it with a pretty fabric. The result is far more cost effective and, frankly, far more comfortable! Now that's what I call a happy accident!

$80

$60

$20

$10

LEFT By painting the existing dresser a glossy white and replacing the hardware with boat cleats, we gave the dated piece a modern update with a subtle nautical wink.

ABOVE AND LEFT When we discovered all the driftwood had come off the mirror in transit, it was all hands on deck. Thankfully, this one-of-a-kind find was shipshape again in no time with a little hot glue.

A Final Thought

The young, energetic newlyweds were more than a little nervous about doing anything "out of the box." Since I don't really do anything "inside the box," they knew they'd have to take a deep breath and just trust us. I understood what they wanted and was confident we'd deliver. I also knew if I told them how we were going to achieve it, they would not be breathing at all—they might faint. Or die. And they would have definitely said no. I would have had to tell them we wanted to paint all their furniture, add metal pipes to their bed to make it taller, paint their floors with wide stripes, and use an antique wicker settee busted by my butt. There's an old saying about sausage—"Don't ask how it gets made; just enjoy how delicious it is." Well, that's kind of what was going on here. And boy, did it turn out delicious.

chapter 3

A DASHING DINING ROOM

This couple's dining room had been taken over by their trio of kids, who had commandeered the space and turned it into an art-filled playroom. Now, with the children a bit older, Mom and Dad are hoping to take back the space and make it the dining room they always wished for. They want the toys out and replaced with a grown-up, glamorous vibe where they can host friends and family alike. Since they have never actually used the dining room to dine (except occasionally on the kids' plastic picnic table), they don't have a table or chairs, or any idea where to start.

1

TOYS AND KID
STUFF ARE
EVERYWHERE.

2

THERE'S NO
EXISTING DINING
FURNITURE TO
WORK WITH.

3

THE TWO
DOORWAYS
HAVE CREATED A
QUIRKY CORNER.

The Plan

A journey from playroom to "Pass the champagne, please"

Once we get the kids' stuff out, this room will be a blank slate. It has substantial crown molding and gets great light—perfect for creating a glamorous Hollywood Regency vibe.

On my to-do list:

- Paint the walls a dramatic gray then add picture-frame molding in a glossy white to give the room more drama.

- Incorporate various shades of pink as an accent color to complement the main colors, gray and white.

- Find a round table with leaves so it can be extended into an oval large enough to host their many friends and family members.

- Look for glass, crystal, and silver accents for added sparkle and shine.

- Add tailored window treatments to soften the space and take this cluttered playroom from pandemonium to pretty darn fantastic.

As much as I love kid art, this smorgasbord of color will move to the family room.

It's time to set these dolphin sconces free!

INSPIRATIONS

BELOW Don't be fooled by the fabric—this kidney-shaped settee is a down-filled dream and perfect for creating the Hollywood Regency vibe in the dining room.

ABOVE This English Regency table—a true antique that comes with three leaves—was only $450 because the veneer on the top was badly chipped. The dealer knew that repairing it would cost a fortune, but that didn't stop me from taking this beauty home. I have an idea of how we can make it sparkle without spending a ton.

The Hunt

I'm looking for furniture that reflects the scene-stealing style of the '40s but with a modern twist.

—shopping list—

- Dining table—oval or round to best complement the room's dimensions

- Chairs—a set of at least eight

- Lighting—a chandelier and glamorous sconces

- Storage options—the usual suspects: a sideboard, a chest, and maybe a bar

- Fabric for window treatments

- Mirrors

- Silver accessories

- Something for an awkward corner—maybe a love seat for post-dessert lounging

It's exciting to find a pair of beautiful lamps in great condition. I always recommend buying both, even if you only need one. You'll want the mate someday—trust me! This pair of pink glass '30s table lamps will anchor the sideboard and add a warm glow to the room. They cost just $100 for the pair.

STYLE INSPIRATION: HOLLYWOOD REGENCY

This style evokes drama, whimsy, and true Hollywood glamour. Originating from the set designs of the film world's golden age in the 1930s and '40s, Hollywood Regency can be spotted in movies like Dinner at Eight, High Society, *and* The Women.

Reflective surfaces

Contrasting colors

Greek key motif

Rich, lush textiles—velvet, mohair, and silk

Asian-style furniture and accessories

Faux bamboo—furniture and accessories carved to look like bamboo

Glossy, lacquered pieces

Animal prints

Symmetry

This set of vintage mahogany shield-back dining chairs came from an estate sale. The owner was downsizing and thrilled to see her beloved chairs go to another happy family. Yes, they are a little dated in style (for now), but they are well made, and a steal at $75 each. (Plus, finding a set of ten vintage chairs in great condition isn't easy!)

the big
REVEAL

FROM PLAYROOM TO PURE GLAM! This space is now a sophisticated showstopper with warm grays, glossy whites, and a splash of punchy pink. It features comfortable seating for a dozen adults and even a few kids. And since it offers up glittering accents and reflective surfaces in pure Hollywood Regency fashion, I think Mom and Dad will probably see guests lingering here long after the credits (and dessert carts) roll.

before

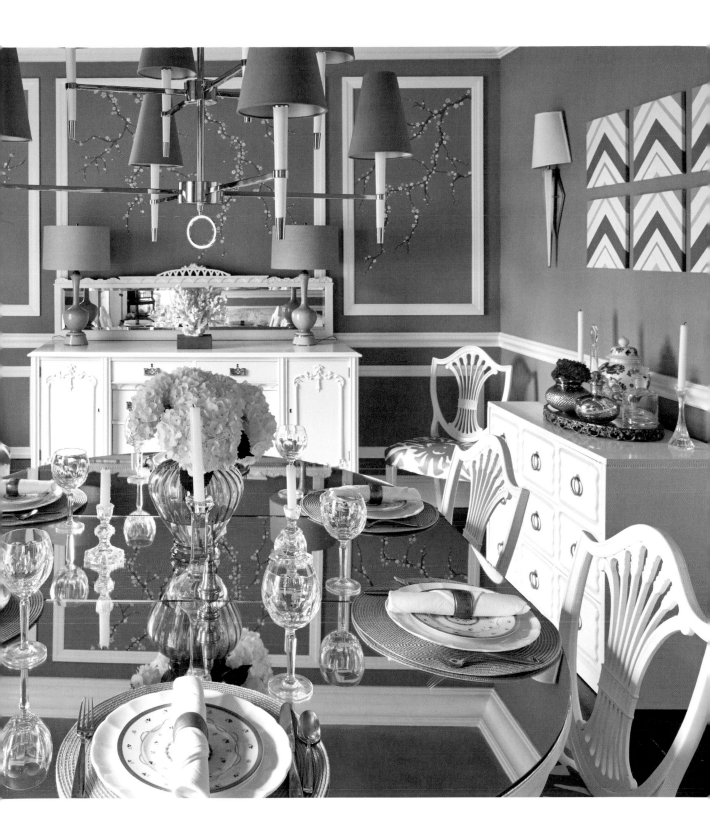

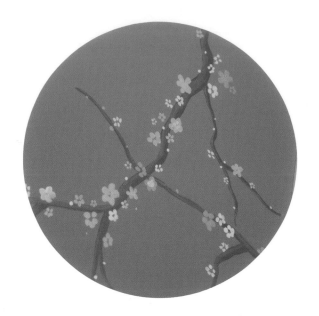

A Room in Bloom

Hand-painted cherry blossoms give this room sophisticated style

We filled this space with unique, artistic touches. The picture-frame molding we added gives the room an architectural, classic look. I placed it on two opposing walls to create symmetry and to frame the cherry blossoms we hand-painted on the wall.

The inspiration for the floral artwork came from one of my all-time favorites—beautiful, hand-painted wallpapers by Gracie. A design company founded in 1898 in New York City, it is legendary for its hand-painted wallcoverings—a blue-blooded favorite that never goes out of style. The panels are beyond elegant, and also extremely expensive. Since they were out of our price range, we decided to take matters into our own hands.

"Before using your walls as a canvas, paint your design on a board first. Practice makes perfect."

—JEN

We sketched our design with pencil and painted our branches first—thicker at the base, and pencil-thin at the tips. The blossoms were created by dabbing five paint dots in a cluster. Multiple shades of pink, gray, and white give the blossoms variation and dimension.

I love this modern chandelier made by Jonathan Adler mixed in with all the antiques!

A SHIMMERY SILVER CEILING

Gray wall paints can appear green, brown, or even lavender, so we tried several shades and looked at them at different times of the day before making our final selection.

For the ceiling, we used Modern Masters Metallic Paint in silver as a base coat. Next, Cija went over the dry silver paint with a mix of water and color tint (a combo of black and umber) to add a smoky, antiqued finish.

To apply, Cija wiped on the mixture in a circular motion with a damp rag, then used a dry rag to wipe off any excess.

RIGHT This nineteenth-century table had a beautifully carved pedestal but the round tabletop was in bad shape. Because it was already in total disrepair, I had no problem painting the ol' girl in glossy white to celebrate her nice curves.

BELOW We used the homeowners' collection of crystal candlesticks to add even more ambiance to the dining table. The mirrored top's reflection creates twice the twinkle!

before

Feast Your Eyes

When I bought this table—a steal for $400 at Black Rock Galleries—its finish was horrific, but its generous size and English Regency style had the potential to become the life of the party. Because of its condition, even painting the top of the table would not mask the imperfections. The solution? A local glass shop cut pieces of mirror to fit perfectly on top of the table and leaves. It amps up the glam factor, and draws light into the space. Situated right beneath the fabulous chandelier, the mirror also doubles the wow factor.

A mirrored table top is sexy!

> ## "Kids have amazing artistic sensibilities. Put a brush in their hand and watch them go!"
>
> **—ALEX**

I chose gray lampshades that seem to disappear into the gray walls—illuminating the hand-painted cherry blossoms without distracting from them.

$95

The kids made this!

We replaced the light-up dolphin sconces with a pair of Art Deco-style stunners found at Build It Green!, a nonprofit salvage yard in New York City.

Pint-Sized Picassos

For years, this family's three children painted artwork and tacked them on the wall—and I didn't want that to completely change. As a surprise to the parents, I had the kids paint chevron strips on canvas using the room's new color palette. The series is a newly minted heirloom and hangs in a place of honor in the dining room.

Go For Gloss

This old sideboard was a big brown beast when I bought it for $150. It was heavy and dark and totally out of date, but I loved it just the same. I could see it actually had great Chinese Chippendale style, with incredible fretwork, an original mirror backsplash, and solid bronze pulls. If it was a "true" antique I would not have painted it, but since it was a later reproduction of a nineteenth-century style, I knew a coat of glossy white woudln't hurt the value and would accentuate the beautiful details.

Hiding under the heavy, brown-black finish were incredible details like carved fretwork, an antique mirror, and solid bronze pulls.

$50

$150

before

"Glossy lacquer can cover a lot of imperfections, but not all. Make sure the surface of your piece is smooth and clean before you paint it."

—MARK

BELOW Exercising my hand-eye coordination while precisely placing the pink ribbon. Just a dab of fabric glue holds it all in place.

Cornice-copia!

A custom cornice with detailing like this one can easily cost you hundreds or even thousands of dollars, but we created a pair for less than $100 each. We made the boxes out of plywood, then wrapped batting and fabric around the front and sides. To add custom detailing, we attached pieces of grosgrain ribbon in a Greek key pattern. (You could also use brass or chrome tacks.) We hung the cornices as high as possible, allowing more light to come in and making the ceilings seem higher—a double win!

The pillow has the same Greek key motif as the cornices!

This vintage faux bamboo mirror had a great shape but a terrible paint job, which is probably why we were able to get it for $40. Sandpaper, primer, and paint were all it took to get it back to fabulous.

before

LEFT AND BELOW Reupholstered in gorgeous gray and white damask-style linen, the vintage settee also delivers a one-two punch of pink on the trim and pillow. It's a great size for an awkward corner and it provides extra seating for kids or an after-dinner cocktail.

before

before

ABOVE Since this Draper chest had already been painted non-traditional colors, I took it one step further and customized it to complement our Hollywood Regency vibe.

LEFT The heavy ring pulls on the Draper chest were dinged up and tired looking, but they were original to the piece, so we used a hammered metallic spray paint to revitalize them.

HISTORY LESSON: DOROTHY DRAPER

The style of the chest in this room is credited to Dorothy Draper—a designer whose work exemplifies the Hollywood Regency style. With a taste for high drama and a revolutionary spirit, Dorothy Draper knew how to make an entrance (or a living room or a dining space, for that matter). Considered the first-ever design professional, Draper—a six-foot-tall decorating goddess—still influences interiors as often today as she did in her heyday in the 1930s, '40s, and '50s.

By steering away from then-popular "period room" styles and infusing spaces with exuberant color combos, gutsy pattern pairings (think chintz with stripes), and glossy floors, mirrors, and ceilings, she broke the design mold—and helped usher in all the glamour that defines Hollywood Regency. Draper's best known for the interiors she created for The Greenbrier resort in West Virginia and the books *Decorating Is Fun!* and *Entertaining Is Fun!*

A Final Thought

As a fellow parent, I could totally feel the homeowners' primary-color-infused pain every time they walked into the dining room. I was also worried how their three kids would take the news that their playroom was being relocated to the basement. Asking them to paint an art piece for the newly decorated space helped them feel involved and very proud. They love the new dining room as much as their parents do, and the best part? Even though they knew the color scheme and saw some of the projects in our workshop beforehand, they kept it all a secret—ensuring a true Hollywood happy ending.

$20

$150

ABOVE A few last-minute tweaks before the family sees the room for the first time!

LEFT The small wooden bar—a yard sale find for $100—is made by Kittinger, a highly collectible mid-century manufacturer.

chapter 4

A WHIMSICAL WOMAN CAVE

This dark basement was filled with a mix of furniture and knickknacks left over from the college days and single lives of two recently engaged women. With their young son in need of a place to play indoors and an upcoming engagement celebration they hope to hold in the space, they need a major upgrade in this depressing dungeon. They'd like it to be a dual-purpose area that serves both as a kids' rec room and a grown-up party space.

1

THE CEILING IS
VERY LOW AND
THERE'S VERY
LITTLE LIGHT.

2

THERE ARE
UNSIGHTLY DUCTS
AND PIPES.

3

THE FURNITURE
IS BULKY AND
NOTHING
MATCHES.

The Plan

Let's banish this basement!

Since this room only has three tiny windows, our first order of business is making it feel light and bright by addressing the dingy walls and ceiling. In addition, the couple also has totally different tastes. One loves geometric patterns in shades of gray, black, and white. Her partner leans more toward feminine prints and softer colors like yellow and blue. My goal is to create a relaxing, cozy destination with a harmonious blend of "her and her" styles.

On my to-do list:

- Replace the massive sectional with a smaller sofa and chairs.

- Brighten up the space with paint, fabrics, and loads of lighting.

- Create a more social layout by breaking up the narrow room into two seating areas so kids and adults can enjoy it at the same time.

- Disguise the unsightly pipes that run across the center of the room and replace the 1970s ceiling tiles.

- Remove the bar that is tucked into a dark corner, and create a new one somewhere else in the room.

The ceiling had stained and missing tiles!

Between the air duct, the low ceiling, and the exposed pipes, we had our hands full.

INSPIRATIONS

ABOVE This flea market find, a '70s groovy metal table, has the right look for the room for $20.

LEFT Always ask the dealer for information on pieces you're interested in—the age, where they found it, and what it was originally used for. This sculpture from the '60s was signed on the bottom by the artist and cost just $35.

The Hunt

We will bring some fun into this space with cool industrial pieces, quirky accessories, and unusual art.

RIGHT This gooseneck lamp with its sculptural shape and '60s vibe was a $5 yard sale find.

FAR RIGHT Inspired! I bought this key art for $10 and plan on creating a supersize version using old keys I bought for $1 apiece.

– shopping list –

- A smaller-scale sofa and chairs

- A cool coffee table big enough for board games

- A vintage bar, or something we can turn into one

- Side tables for drinks and snacks

- A media console to house the TV and electronics, with storage for toys and games

- Lamps, lamps, and more lamps!

- Funky accessories for the built-in bookshelves

TOP LEFT I don't need a dresser for this space but I do need a media console with storage—and the size of this piece is ideal. For $80, we'll give it a makeover and put it to good use!

LEFT We'll mix metals, shapes, and styles in this eclectic room—adding pieces like this wicker table that cost just $15.

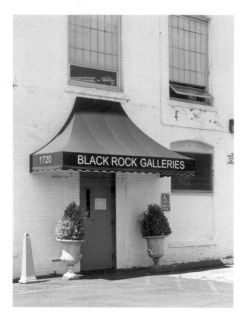

RIGHT Black Rock Galleries is one of my favorite shops. Its 20,000 square feet of treasures and junk is pure paradise, if you don't mind digging!

FAR RIGHT Tying one on at Tiger Lily's in Greenwich, Connecticut, as we hunt for fun fabrics.

Wouldn't this make a fabulous chandelier?

STYLE INSPIRATION: FEMININE INDUSTRIAL

Need to blend two styles? Make up your own! That's what we did in this space when we merged geometric shapes with soft fabrics and accessories. Some of the elements include:

Pops of classic industrial colors like safety yellow and red mixed with soft blues and grays

Vintage factory equipment and tools transformed into usable furniture

Raw or unfinished surfaces with texture and patina (chipping and rust included)

Fabrics and cushioning in florals, geometrics, and solid colors

Quirky art, old tin toys, game pieces

BELOW This vintage fire extinguisher mounted as a lamp has a cool industrial look and since the homeowner's dad happens to be a firefighter, it's both stylish *and* sentimental.

Serve it up! Vintage wooden racquets are obsolete on tennis courts today, but the patina and graphics can be a grand slam as wall art. These were $3 apiece!

An antique door for $100. Love the original paint!

ABOVE Elephant's Trunk Flea Market in New Milford, Connecticut, is the real deal. It's huge and packed with amazing finds.

LEFT Knock, knock. Who's there? An antique door salvaged from a nineteenth-century house. It's the perfect height and width to become a beautiful bar front!

SECONDHAND STATS

The first flea market in America was in Canton, Texas, in 1873.

the big REVEAL

THEY SAY OPPOSITES ATTRACT and that certainly was the case here. By mixing industrial and mid-century pieces and adding a dash of girl power to soften the edges, we gave this couple a new style that's all their own. The furniture, art, and quirky accessories all say something about each of them: one of a kind and fabulous. Who'd have though the horrible basement would become one of the most-loved spots in the house. Bring on the little-kid playdates and big-kid parties! The woman cave is open for business!

before

before

Cija and Alex installed our custom floating shelves to make the pipes seem to disappear!

Now You See Them . . . Now You Don't!

Exposed pipes look great in the right space— like a nineteenth-century New York City loft. Unfortunately, they don't have quite the same appeal in this '50s-era basement. The party lights strung on the pipes to "pretty them up" aren't helping matters.

Since construction wasn't an option to hide pipes and ducts, the team created a way to hide them in plain sight. First we painted them the same shade of soft gray-blue that we used on the walls. Then we made plywood shelves to run the length of the wall and mounted them above and below the pipes. Painted in a brilliant shade of blue, they are so eye-catching that you don't even notice those pesky pipes that run parallel.

"Rustic furniture can have splinters or exposed nails. Make sure to give it a thorough once-over to ensure that it's safe."

—DAVID

A hundred-year-old industrial cart from Brimfield made a fabulous coffee table once we tapped in the old nails, sanded the wood, and sealed it with a coat of clear shellac.

Remember the pipes?
Wait . . . where'd they go?

$45

$40

$100

before

I'd never seen anything like this turn-of-the-century chaise. It's great for a snooze or as multi-person seating.

The high-gloss white paint makes the carved details pop!

Fabric Fake-Out

Curtains are a fantastic way to soften a space, but when your window is only 14 inches tall, the last thing you want to do is cover it. Instead, we decided to have curtains flank the entertainment center to make the room more sophisticated and feminine. Covering two large portions of the wall from floor to ceiling, the drapes added height and concealed a lot of the piping along that wall. Combined with the placement of the media console, TV, and the quirky wooden swordfish/orca that is most certainly one of a kind, this space is now quite a catch.

BELOW AND RIGHT David, our resident "electrifier," helping me turn these industrial stanchions into truly unique standing lamps.

$15

$150

$80

To convert the ugly $80 dresser into a media console, we drilled a hole in the back to allow for cables and wires, and took out the top row of drawers to make room for the electronics. Painted glossy gray, it's hard to believe it once belonged in a bedroom!

before

We glued the same wallpaper on this tabletop for an easy update!

Oval mirrors glued to the strings make these racquets a grand slam!

Pretty Shiny Things

The room's built-in bookshelves were a great scale and offered a ton of storage. Unfortunately, they were painted pitch black, which made the space seem even darker. To brighten them up, we primed and painted them white and then hung a geometric wallpaper by Jonathan Adler on the back wall. The metallic pattern reflects light and adds a touch of glamour to the space. The project only took one roll of paper, so it was totally affordable—major bang for the buck!

"The ceiling is like your fifth wall! Don't neglect it, especially in a room with low ceilings."

—ALEX

$25

This is where the bar used to be!

$25

TOP For this space, we chose a geometric but curved pattern, a great compromise for the couple's differing tastes.

MIDDLE These tiles are light as air and a cinch to cut to size using either a blade or scissors.

BOTTOM Alex used paper to cut templates for the tiles that had pipe holes or complex shapes.

On the Up-and-Up

The dropped ceiling was covered in stained acoustic tiles from the '70s, but with no budget to "raise the roof" so to speak, we searched for a simpler solution. Thin foam tiles we bought from decorativeceilingtiles.com are easy to cut to size and simple to install using ceramic tile adhesive. Their pearly sheen is light reflective and they come in a variety of designs. The team glued them right over the old acoustic tiles, and in just a few hours, we had what looked like a brand-new ceiling.

$100

BELOW My heart skipped a beat when I spied this humorously cool sign, an eye-popping combo of industrial and pop art. After the team cleaned him up and electrified him using colored bulbs, he was lovingly christened "Bob" the bartender.

before

What a man! David installs wiring to bring the sign to life and add yet another source of light to the space.

Key to Her Heart

I made sure the art in this space reflected the couple's personalities. They're both really fun and hip, so the pieces I chose for them are one-of-a-kind and a bit offbeat.

My favorite is one we made ourselves—a large pink backdrop with a heart made of keys to celebrate the couple's love for each other.

Vintage keys can be a dime a dozen at flea markets—literally. I picked up 40 keys in different finishes and sizes, an old frame (an estate-sale find for $5), and a remnant of pink velvet, which we glued on to the backing using spray adhesive. Then we dumped the keys onto a table and moved them around until they formed a perfect heart. For under $30, we created a custom piece that was sweet, stylish, and sentimental.

Look for old keys at flea markets!

$10

$5

That's a lot of Chiclets. (And patience!)

TOP Covering a piece of plywood with pink velvet is as easy as wrapping a present.

ABOVE Jen and I used vintage keys to form a heart shape. You can also create a peace sign, a smiley face, or your monogram!

LEFT Who knew the contents of your trick-or-treat bag could be so artful? This one-of-a-kind art piece is made of vintage Chiclets boxes glued together and framed. Below, the '60s aluminum bar cart holds vintage barware.

BELOW Just $1 apiece at the Brooklyn Flea Market in New York City, these bingo cards were turned into a great piece of graphic art. We cut out yellow circles to resemble game chips, glued them to construction paper, and placed them in a vintage frame.

$100

$125

ABOVE David and Alex built a bar incorporating the $100 antique door we found at a flea market. The original paint on the door was in great shape—all it needed was a good cleaning. We even kept the knob to hang purses or coats!

Hey, Bartender

When the couple moved into this house, it came with an ill-fitting bar that was so massive, party guests could barely reach across to get their drinks. What's more, the bar was tucked away from view of the television. (And what's the point of grabbing a beer during a ball game if you can't see the score on the TV screen?)

Our solution: Remove the old bar and create a new one facing the opposite direction so both the guests and server can see the TV. The starting point for the new structure came from our flea-found blue door, which became the bar front. The team built the rest of the bar around the door's dimensions using plywood and painted it the same shade of blue. We added three vintage stools (a Brimfield find) and some vintage barware, and topped it off with our hunky light-up bartender, Bob.

Open-and-Shut Case

Moving the bar to the opposite side of the room placed it in front of a damp cellar that was too scary to use even as storage. I immediately saw it as an ideal opportunity for a chic wine cellar that would complement the new bar and add storage.

The stars aligned with this project, as we came up with tons of clever ideas for turning the cellar around (literally!), starting with the door—which we took off the hinges and hung to open the other way so it didn't obstruct the flow of traffic in the room.

David built a plywood base with storage cubbies, then stacked clay chimney pots from a building-supply store to house the wine. To showcase the reclaimed space, we cut a window in the door, installed glass, and then painted it a sunny yellow. It's definitely a solution worth toasting!

"The temperature in small below-ground areas like these is typically around 60 degrees—perfect for wine storage!"

—DAVID

These are chimney pots!

LEFT The couple hated this unfinished, scary-looking cellar that served no purpose other than to creep them out.

before

Let there be light! A metal carriage wheel is now a chandelier.

LEFT This oddly shaped nook that once housed the bar area was turned into a daybed where friends can hang out by the new bar, or stay the night after a great party! We upholstered the walls and added curtain panels for an extra-inviting touch of elegance. The steel wheel used for the light was just $20. It cost David another $10 to wire it.

BOTTOM A circular patterned fabric fit perfectly on these stools that now flank the couple's antique game table. We also painted some game pieces to add a pop to playtime.

before

We painted chess pieces to match the color scheme!

$20

before

Prints Charming

Don't be paranoid by pattern!

We took this dark basement to a whole new level by spreading several cheerful prints and patterns throughout the room. Sam and her mom, Betsy, who own Tiger Lily's in Greenwich, Connecticut, helped me find just the right mix of fabrics to use for the furniture, curtains, pillows, and even for the upholstered walls surrounding the daybed.

It's fun to use several patterns as long as you mix up the scale. Large, medium, and small print fabrics can blend beautifully. If you're nervous about mixing it up, use solid fabrics on larger pieces like sofas and busier prints on chairs, stools, and pillows.

A Final Thought

We attacked this dismal dungeon from top to bottom—the ceiling, the pipes, the bar, the creepy storage space—and managed to upgrade it all! Of all the projects the team took on, though, I absolutely love the daybed tucked in the back corner of the room. It's the perfect spot to take a snooze or read a book. I also need to give a massive shout-out to David for turning the scary cellar into a cool and chic wine cooler. I mean, who'd ever think of using chimney pots as wine-bottle holders? Genius! And let me tell you, by the time we finished this space (which was by far the most challenging in this book), we all needed a glass of vino—or two. Or three. Cheers to the best Woman Cave ever!

chapter 5

A DYNAMIC DEN

This room was the family's favorite—that is, until it flooded and had to be cleared out. When they moved to higher ground and created a new den upstairs, they left this lower-level lair to become a has-been habitat, collecting depressed old furniture and knickknacks. Now that their kids are grown up and moving out, the homeowners are ready to clear out the clutter. They recently added a bar in the room adjacent, so this would be the ideal spot for guest to bring their drinks, gather round the fireplace, and relax.

THE DESIGN DILEMMA

1

WATER DAMAGE FORCED THE FAMILY TO DESERT THE ROOM.

2

IT HAS LOW CEILINGS, SMALL WINDOWS, AND AN ODD LEDGE.

3

WE MUST REUSE SENTIMENTAL PIECES.

The Plan

From storage room to simply stunning!

The husband says he wants an eclectic look and the wife wants "French Country," but here's the thing—neither one of them could describe exactly what they meant. The great news was, they were totally open to anything, and agreed on using shades of brown and orange—with accessories inspired by nature. Their home is set in a wooded area, so the earthtones will work perfectly.

On my to-do list:

- Reuse some of the homeowners' stuff—like a cool rocking chair and a pair of settees that are so ugly I feel I must transform them.

- Create a main seating area in front of the fireplace and do something totally amazing to the wall behind it to make it the focal point.

- Make the room feel like an earthly delight, with art, accessories, and fabrics that all play into a nature theme.

- Lighten up the dark space with some fabulous mirrors and lamps. The more the merrier!

Our color palette was inspired by this seascape, painted by Grandpa!

This room used to be a favorite, but eventually became a catch-all for all of the family's unused furniture.

INSPIRATIONS

BELOW No, these are not mangled rakes. They're a pair of wall sculptures that look like bunches of tall grass. Sam and I bought them for $12 at the Elephant's Trunk Flea Market.

ABOVE This pair of extra-tall brass candlesticks came out of a church and only cost $25. Amen to that!

The Hunt

Browns, beiges, and oranges—oh my! Gold tone accessories and anything with an animal motif will be seriously considered. This room is going to be WILD when we are done with it.

This ottoman was in awful shape, but with its classic lines and size—spot on for the space—and a $5 asking price, it was all mine! A piece like this is perfect for kicking up your feet, or as extra seating if last-minute guests arrive.

BELOW This 1960s gold metal stool is perfect for hiding electronics and wires underneath a console I plan to use in the space.

Flea markets are the best for inexpensive accessories!

Good Bones!

ABOVE Flea markets always have piles of vintage frames that usually cost next to nothing! We'll use them to frame the family's own paintings.

TOP This '70s buffet and matching huntboard, part of a dining set, were only $50 apiece at an estate sale. They are boring brown right now, but paint will make them look modern and fresh!

HOW TO MIX & MATCH

The styles of the pieces I bought for this room run the gamut—from French to downright mid-century funky! So how do I know it will all work together? Here's what I think about when putting together a Flea Market Fabulous room.

1. Assess what you have to work with. Most rooms will have one or two pieces that will act as jumping-off points. Take pictures of them with your smartphone and write down measurements. You want to look for shapes and materials that complement what you already have.

2. Pick accessories that have a similar theme. In this case, I will look for anything that feels like it represents nature in color, texture, or subject matter.

3. Don't be afraid to mix metals. Brass candlesticks, gold frames, and bronze figurines will all unite the furniture pieces they adorn.

4. The more eclectic your furniture plan, the more simple the flooring. A natural-fiber rug keeps things grounded.

the big REVEAL

I DARE THIS COUPLE to ever desert this space again! In fact, I bet they won't be able to pull themselves away from it. Loaded with cool finds and awesome ideas, it's eclectic for him, rustic and cozy for her, and inviting for all who enter. The room is the perfect place to gather, celebrate, or simply chill out. It's got bold, luxurious layers of pattern and a punch of personality!

before

The Heart of the Room

This recessed fireplace wall gets the royal treatment

The fireplace wall Jen designed was, in a word, HOT. Sorry to be cliché, but the orange fabric with the brushed brass tacks in an elaborate X pattern turns up the heat in a big way! We created it using foam core panels you can get at any art supply store. We covered them with orange linen fabric using spray adhesive; and because the foam core is so soft, we just pushed in the tacks with our fingers.

Cija built the simple wood mantel using a chunky piece of poplar she cut to size, stained, and mounted on a 2-by-4-inch cleat. We mounted brass sconces with articulated arms on either side and opted for no artwork between them, since the wall itself was such a masterpiece!

> "The foam core we used in this project can also be used to make window cornices. Embellish them with furniture tacks arranged in a pattern or monogram."
>
> —JEN

before

$30

$60

Raising Cane

Don't let busted seats scare you away—you might miss out on a beautiful bargain, like these bentwood armchairs I bought for just $40. Rather than replace the caning, which can be pricey, we cut out plywood, bought some foam and four yards of fabric, and gave them a brand-new look. Painted matte gray and covered in a tribal print, they look classic with a modern twist. (And they are way more comfortable to sit in!)

After we painted the chairs gray, we sanded the edges to "age" them. Using just two yards of fabric per chair, we upholstered the inserts.

before

Create a series of prints using pages of an old coffee table book!

$12

$50

$65

$190

$25

$150

The coffee table—$40!

For Plants or a Pop!

This coffee table was a first for me—I have never seen one that is so party-ready with its own built-in cooler. In all likelihood, the copper insert was probably put in for plants, which is how I would use it—that is unless I was having a party. Then I would fill it with ice and wine and whatever else my guests are drinking. All it needed was a little TLC—namely, a good sanding, and a rubdown with wood wax, and it is now the toast of the room!

ABOVE Cija puts me to work waxing the table to bring out its warm luster and sheen.

TOP Vary the heights of your tabletop accessories. Here, I put a wide-bodied elephant and a big fern alongside a pair of narrow candlesticks. It's more appealing to the eye, and you don't want guests to gloss over and miss any of your cool finds.

If the small painting was to fill out the large ornate frame, it would need a little help. We cut a mat out of wood to bridge the gap and covered it with a fabric—creating a custom mat that cost next to nothing.

A frame now worthy of the family's beloved painting!

Picture This

The homeowner's father painted a seascape that meant the world to the family, and asked that we included it in the room. If it was going to hold a place of importance, though, it would need a more substantial frame. I found a nineteenth-century carved and gilded beauty that was still in amazing shape. Its opening was too big for the piece, but it's easy to cut down a frame or in this case, fill up the space using a mat. A great antique frame like this makes any artwork look more important, and it was a steal for just $40.

ABOVE AND LEFT David answered my prayers for great lighting, turning our church candlesticks into masterful table lamps. He simply drilled a hole in the tops and ran wiring down the hollow shafts. We topped them with crisp white lampshades.

"When you're looking for something unique to turn into a lamp, go for something that's hollow so it's easy to run the wire through."

—DAVID

LEFT The pair of '60s clover-shaped side tables has brass detailing and beautifully carved legs, but the tops were in bad shape. Painting them tangerine was much more cost-effective than stripping and re-staining. We didn't paint the legs—the wood finish makes the tops pop even more.

before

BELOW The homeowners' existing settees were a sorry state of appairs, so we toned them down and re-covered them in a subtle gray print.

BOTTOM Did you know you can change the shape of a couch or chair? You can! The dipped back and carved frame are gone in the picture below.

before

Love (These) Seats

Who doesn't love a good comeback story? The family was ready to ditch a pair of "French" style settees that had been left by an aunt, but we saw something in them, and just knew we could transform them from tacky to terrific. At Sam's upholstery shop, the backs were built up with plywood and foam to straighten the overly curvy backs and make them feel a little more modern. The nasty fabric was replaced with a subtle geometric pattern, and now the settees are nothing short of *fantastique*!

"A sofa with very straight lines is ideal for a large-scale pattern."

—SAM

SLEEPING BEAUTY

How we woke up a vintage sofa sleeper!

The sofa to the left was only $150—an amazing price considering its down cushions and faux bamboo carved frame. Then I realized why it was such a good deal: It weighed a ton—loaded down with a built-in bed no one in their right mind would want to haul home.

Sofa beds are the ugly stepchildren of secondhand sofas. Nobody wants to sit where someone else has slept! But thankfully you don't have to. Sam's team at Tiger Lily's pulled out the folding mattress and mechanics (not that it was simple—it took two guys to do it), and cut a piece of thick plywood to create a new bench. They secured it in place and reupholstered everything in a big and bold fabric by Robert Allen. I normally prefer a solid on the larger pieces in a room (this was a gutsy move) but the settees—in a much smaller Robert Allen pattern—act as a great balance.

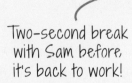

Two-second break with Sam before it's back to work!

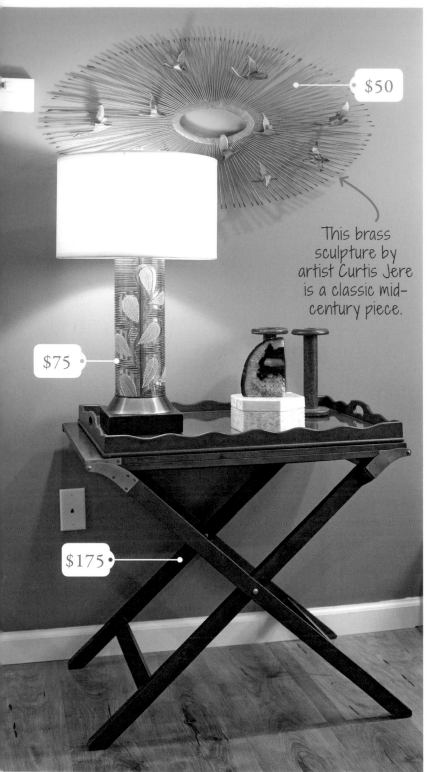

$50

This brass sculpture by artist Curtis Jere is a classic mid-century piece.

$75

$175

"If a piece has a label by a respected manufacturer, check with an antique appraiser to see if refinishing it would decrease its value."

—MARK

LEFT The hand-painted leaves on the '60s lamp charmed me at a charity thrift shop. The botanical theme and colors are perfect for the room.

BELOW What's better than a functionally fabulous butler's tray? This vintage piece, found at an estate sale in Connecticut, does triple duty—it can be a regular-size table or an extra-long console. The tray also lifts off and can be used separately!

before

RIGHT We found a piece of cowhide at a flea market for $35. It was too small to be a rug, but perfect for re-covering the $5 footstool I bought at a yard sale. The result? An awesome ottoman that cost a total of $40!

BELOW The footstool was originally covered in filthy felt and tarnished nailheads. Even though it had to be completely reinvented, the brass tacks inspired our fireplace surround project.

$5

A Final Thought

It's always fun decorating a room for people who aren't afraid to go for it. Color, pattern, style, you name it—this couple was open to it all. I also loved the fact that the mom was a fellow Penn State graduate. I considered using navy blue and white, our school colors, as a nod to our alma mater. While I know my fellow Nittany Lion would have loved it, we had to consider the other rooms around it. They all don't have to match perfectly, but they should have a common thread so that the spaces flow smoothly from one to the other. In this case, it was all about warm tones ranging from yellows to browns to orange. It's now a room that seems to call out for a hearty glass of red wine from the bar next door, and will never again be left in the dust.

chapter 6

A POSH PARLOR

These newlyweds learned a lesson in economics the hard way: They bought a house thinking they would fix it up and flip it. When the market took a turn for the worse, however, they decided to move in and make it their own. They wanted to add color, personality, and style. He likes modern and trendy, but she's more traditional—and they had no idea how to compromise in the parlor of their Victorian-era home. Since it's the first room guests see when entering the house, it had to be beautiful, but it also had to function as a comfortable spot to hang out and watch TV. That's not an easy combination in any space, and this one certainly had its share of challenges.

1

THE ROOM IS
SMALL AND
ASYMMETRICAL.

2

WALL SPACE IS
LIMITED, MAKING
IT DIFFICULT TO
PERSONALIZE
WITH ART.

3

THE SOFA
EATS UP THE
ENTIRE ROOM.

The Plan

Making a fab first impression with flea market finds

I've designed lots of rooms in my time, and could see why this space was tricky for the homeowners. For starters, there was zero symmetry, thanks to two doorways, a giant bay window, and one odd, off-centered window on a large wall. The plan is to create a killer focal point so stunning, it makes you forget about all those quirks. We'll also use lots of pairs of things—like tables, lamps, and accessories—to create a sense of balance that currently doesn't exist.

On my to-do list:

- Find ways to make the room seem taller, larger, and easier to maneuver.

- Turn one wall into a high-impact focal point.

- Offer more seating solutions in the right scale for the space.

- Find some fun, funky tables and accessories.

- Replace the outdated ceiling fan with a stylish chandelier, and add lamps all around for more light.

Time for the fish to swim upstream
(to the husband's home office)!

Unsure of what to do, the couple settled in neutral territory: beige walls and a big (really, REALLY big) brown sectional that seems to swallow this space.

INSPIRATIONS

RIGHT I admit I have a chair addiction. When I see a cute or quirky seat, I have a hard time saying no. Negotiated down to $18, this piece had gothic style—carved legs and a tall, rounded back that may have been an ironing board or surfboard in a former life.

BELOW A flea market find for $40, this pair of armchairs was a reminder that "they don't make 'em like they used to." Compact and very comfortable, the club chairs swiveled and rocked. Yes, they desperately needed new fabric, but even with the cost of reupholstery, they would be a super addition to the room at a super low price.

THE POWER OF PAIRS

Finding one foo dog at a flea market is fun. Finding two? Tremendous! I buy 'em every chance I can. A pair of almost anything is a plus, because it helps create symmetry in a room. Be on the lookout for pairs of:

Cozy chairs

Mirrors

Foo dogs

Pretty vases

Vintage art prints

Sconces

Lamps

The Hunt

This house may date to Victorian times, but I'm looking for pieces that will create a modern yet classic look.

I have to replace the couple's big brown sectional, which takes up way too much space in the room. I know this may not look like an upgrade, but it is in a major way! Unde the faded green fabric is a classic tuxedo style frame that will look fabulous when it's reupholstered.

LEFT I got this quirky triangular coffee table for $60 at a Housing Works thrift shop in New York City. It was peeking out from beneath a console—if I hadn't been willing to dig, I never would have seen its distinctive shape.

Antiques OPEN "Stop In & Browse"

— shopping list —

- Sofa and pair of club chairs that are the right size for the petite parlor

- Lots of lighting—a chandelier, table lamps, and maybe a standing lamp

- A coffee table

- Storage—tables, shelves, whatever might work

- Window treatments—to soften the space and add privacy

- Accessories that add style and personality

SECONDHAND STATS

The longest yard sale in the USA is the 127 Corridor—an annual 690-mile-event that starts 5 miles north of Addison, Michigan, and goes all the way down to Gadsden, Alabama.

RIGHT The ceiling fan in the parlor is being replaced with a more modern chandelier, but the couple still wants air to circulate. Our stylish solution? I'll buy a vintage table fan that has a great industrial look and ask David to rewire it to ensure it works properly.

the big REVEAL

MODERN WITH A CLASSIC TWIST, the couple's parlor now greets guests with a warm welcome. There's double the amount of seating than before and yet it looks much bigger because of the scale of the furniture and the way it's arranged. Best of all we were able to conquer the room's off-kilter quality, creating balance with pairs of items, ignoring the quirky architecture when placing pieces, and turning a wall into a singular, sensational piece of art. Asymmetry never looked so good!

before

A mix of table and floor lamps ensures even lighting!

$15

$20

$60

> "A bold wall treatment can downplay unusual architecture in a room."
>
> —CIJA

If These Walls Could Talk

At first, I thought the room's walls were working against us—especially when it came to figuring out where to hang art. There were three main walls, and one was dedicated to the couple's TV. The largest had an off-kilter window so if we hung any artwork it would never look centered no matter where we put it.

The solution was risky—we decided to pretend the window wasn't there and just turn the entire wall into one giant art piece! Cija and Jen created an ingenious three-dimensional design that uses strips of plywood, paint, and remnants of wallpaper. The result is a geometric dream that gives the husband the mod vibe he wanted as well as the soft color palette his wife adores.

Apple-green table skirts with a sexy center slit help dress up a simple pair of round tables. The Greek key pattern complements the design on the curtain trim.

The green sofa, bought for just $70 at an estate sale, is now covered in linen with details on the cushions.

before

"Nowadays, paint stores can color match almost anything. You can bring a favorite fabric, an art piece, or a bookcover, and have that exact hue made."

—ALEX

RIGHT *Au revoir*, outdated finish. A gold spray-painted étagère—a $50 yard sale find—got an instant update when Alex painted it coral. Becuase it's got minimal surface area, it's a safe way to add an unexpected pop of color.

$40

$50

$18

before

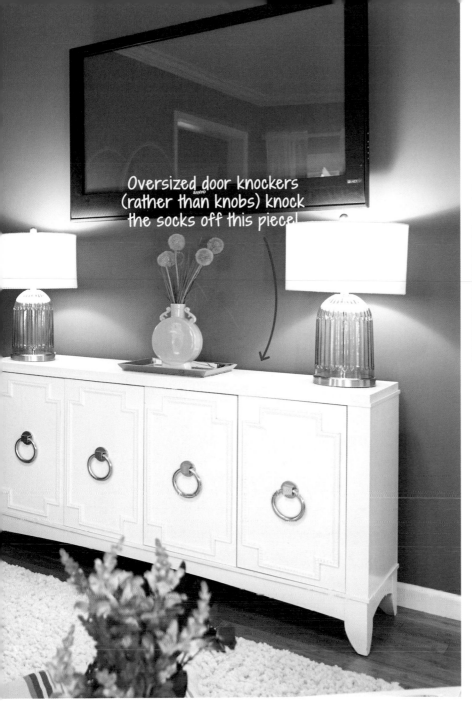

Oversized door knockers (rather than knobs) knock the socks off this piece!

BELOW Adding store-bought molding to a generic piece costs next to nothing and adds so much style.

before

A Total Knockout

The scale of the couple's existing console (pictured above) was spot on, but its style was a bit generic. We changed that, giving the piece a custom look by using wood molding from a hardware store to create a frame on each of the doors and then painted it glossy white, and also swapped out the existing hardware with hefty door knockers for a more substantial look.

A deco-style chrome chandelier is much cooler than the ceiling fan it replaced.

$20

We got rid of the tufting on the backs of the armchairs and replaced the dated blue velvet with a fresh, large-scale floral pattern.

before

We added this Greek key trim to plain store-bought curtain panels!

$125

$60

$20

Floor pillows serve as extra seating— comfy on the new plush shag rug!

ABOVE I knew this quirky triangle coffee table would come to life once we painted it white—but it turned out even better than I had imagined! The metal frame took on a lattice-like feel, and the three-sided shape is a perfect complement to the softer edges on the other pieces.

A Final Thought

The award for best reaction by the homeowners goes to . . . this amazing couple, who screamed for what felt like a full five minutes when they walked in the room. They were so happy, and that made us so happy. Little did they know, getting their small room to look so stylish was a gigantic pain in the . . . asymmetry! What you can't tell from the pictures is that we moved the furniture around five or six times before we settled on the floor plan you just saw on these pages. Originally we thought we'd put the sofa in the window, and there was a desk in the mix that was eventually edited out. It all worked in the end—but let's just say there was no need for the gym after this makeover. But the best part? Every single piece we ended up using—the club chairs, the sofa, the coffee table, and even the couple's own console—all rescued, recycled, or reimagined—are even better the second time around!

chapter 7

A MEGA-WATT
MEDIA ROOM

Sometimes the constraints of a room—its shape, size, lighting, or lack thereof—get you stuck in a rut. Such was the case for this family. Their lower-level space had stained plaster walls, low ceilings, and a drainage pipe smack-dab in the center of the room. Unsure of what to do with the odd space, they chose to do nothing, and the room quickly morphed into a dumping ground for tools, crafts, long-abandoned toys, and a collection of more than 250 VHS tapes. Overwhelmed by what it had become, they asked me to help get it back on track and realize all it could be.

The Plan

Uniting a room divided

Since this media room is not ready for its close-up—let alone any kind of family activities—we will start by clearing out *everything*. The only exceptions are the two items the family asked to incorporate: a pair of colorful Carnival masks from their native Dominican Republic, and a bolt of fabric the mother bought and absolutely adored but never used.

On my to-do list:

- Create a space for the family to gather together to watch movies and get their game on.

- Remove the shelving around the pipe in the center of the room.

- Incorporate a bolt of fabric the mother bought but never knew how to use.

- Replace the shower curtain hanging in the doorway leading to the laundry room with a door of some kind.

- Set a groovy, journeyed tone through textured, patterned, and deeply hued designs.

The aim of this room divider was to create storage for books, movies, games, and a projector for a ceiling-mounted screen, but it wound up just being a catch-all that made the room feel small and cramped.

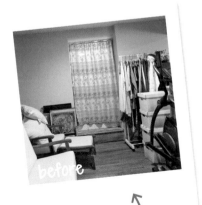

No, that's not a shower. The laundry room is behind the curtain!

INSPIRATIONS

BELOW The family had no comfortable seating for their media room. This perfect pair came out of a home where the furniture was covered in plastic so there's no need to recover. (Thanks, Grandma!)

The Hunt

Despite the fact that the room was packed to the gills, there wasn't much to work with. You know what that means: a major shopportunity!

ABOVE Just $100 for the set of four, these '60s bridge chairs are collapsible and have great mid-century lines.

– shopping list –

- Seating—a sofa and chairs

- Coffee table and side tables

- Lighting

- Storage ideas

- Accessories—the more exotic, the better

- Anything to encourage and complement the family's hobbies

ABOVE Vintage kilim rugs are great for layering on a wood floor for a Park Avenue or bohemian look. If they are too beat up, cut and sew them into pillows.

RIGHT Because this 1920s console was dark and heavy looking and the wood veneer top was peeling, I was able to buy it for just $30!

ABOVE This old card table didn't look like much, but it will be perfect for board games, and its flat gray paint job is a blank canvas for us to create something special.

ABOVE I scored this china cabinet, an end-of-day estate-sale find, for just $50. Part of a set, I bought all three pieces, all of which I've used in this book!

RIGHT It's no wonder my favorite flea market is called Elephant's Trunk. I always snap up cool finds like this big-eared elephant.

SECONDHAND STATS

The largest flea market in the world? The Brimfield Antique Show in Brimfield, Massachusetts. As many as 6,000 dealers sell their wares there three times each year!

the big
REVEAL

WHAT WAS ORIGINALLY A CLUTTERED storage space with zero direction is now a warm, eclectic room that screams "festive and fun"! The theme organically morphed into '70s Morocco, thanks to the family's favorite fabric and a few chic vintage finds. Mom and Dad can now entertain or have a romantic movie night. Their teenage daughter can have friends over, cozy up with a book, or do homework. An inviting space with a very groovy vibe, it's a cool crib that prioritizes playtime.

before

To conceal the retractable screen, we built a cornice and covered it in the same wallpaper we used on the walls!

A leather panel hides the chipped console top!

$20

$10

A Clever Console Cover-Up

Creating a leather table top in under a half hour!

Since we removed the shelving that spliced the room in two, we needed to find someplace else to store electronics, DVDs, and knickknacks. The solution was a 1920s console that fits beautifully under the large window. The body of the piece was in fine shape, but the top had serious water damage. To repair it, we simply stripped off the damaged veneer and sanded down the plywood underneath. Once it was super smooth, we covered the top with a new piece of cocoa-colored faux leather. Brass tacks secure it in place and tie in with the other gold tone accents.

$15

$25

Dynamic Duo

Check out the below photo of a serious diamond in the rough! Actually, it doesn't get any rougher. I had a hunch this nineteenth-century club chair had nice bones hiding somewhere under the layers of ancient fabric and exposed springs. For just $15 at Brimfield, it was worth finding out.

I found a similar single club chair (also below) at an estate sale for $20 and created an almost perfect pair by using the same fabrics: a durable faux leather on the back and arms (where chairs take the biggest beating) and a pricey paisley down the middle. Mixing-and-matching is an inexpensive way to get a luxe, custom-made look for less. Just another reason I love rescuing and reinventing secondhand scores!

before

These were rebuilt and reupholstered to look like a pair!

"If you love a fabric that's really expensive, mix and match it with something more affordable to create two-toned custom furniture!"

—SAM

before

$5

$35

After removing the parts from a vintage TV, we added shelving and repurposed it as a cocktail table with storage for electronics!

"Retro repurposing projects like this TV side table add nostalgia and humor to a room."

—CIJA

BELOW Cija and I are ready for our close-up.

Totally Tubular

A vintage TV from the '50s gets a second chance as a side table with storage below. When I spotted this at a yard sale, the owner was thrilled that I wanted to give him anything for it!

The outside of the TV was perfect—the original graphics and black paint untouched—but the heavy mechanics inside had to be gutted. After removing the parts and the lens, we made shelves for the shelled-out interior to house the DVD player and VCR—the perfect way to meld the past and present with one-of-a-kind design.

Hidden behind the curtain of the "Moroccan" cabinet—the family's massive collection of VHS tapes!

before

ABOVE To spice up this boring cabinet, we took the doors off and covered up the traditional molding with a plywood cutout inspired by Moorish architecture.

You've Got Game!

We used green painter's tape (specifically made for delicate surfaces) to map out a design on the top of our $20 table, then we painted it in three shades that coordinate with the rest of the room. It is now the perfect spot for a mean game of gin rummy or a Monopoly marathon.

before

$150

$25

ABOVE We spray painted the card table in ivory. Jen mapped out the geometric design in pencil and used painter's tape to create razor-sharp lines between the shades of orange and gold.

LEFT The orange vinyl seats on the '50s collapsible bridge chairs were in good condition and the perfect scale for the game table—all we needed to do was paint the wood frames glossy white.

Magic Carpet

We transformed thrift-store slipper chairs into stunning stools that are useful as extra seating when company comes to visit. They can also be used as side tables with a tray placed atop. (Talk about working overtime!)

To create the stools, we removed the backs of the chairs and covered the seats with vintage Persian rugs. They had rips and tears so we were happy to cut them up and give them a second chance as stools.

These stools used to be chairs!

before

ABOVE In the midst of the clutter, we found a terrific vintage treasure the family had forgotten about: a 1970s Japanese pachinko machine. This pinball-like game delivers a retro feel that is in keeping with our theme and color palette. The piece is no longer working but it's still very much in play as a piece of artwork.

Webbing was a simple and chic solution to hide the seams. The upholstery tacks hold it all together— and look divine!

A Splash of Color

The family used to have a shower curtain hanging in the doorway leading to the adjacent laundry room. It had to go, but the question was how to partition the space without a swinging door (there was no room). The solution: creating a Moroccan-inspired entrance using a secondhand bifold door from a salvage yard. We painted layers of royal blue over brick red to create a "painted many times" look. We then added extra-large upholstery tacks to accentuate the raised panels. The door was mounted on a barn door–style track that allows it to slide left to right.

The royal blue color is also sprinkled throughout the rest of the room. The rich shade creates a vibrant contrast to our warm red and orange tones.

ABOVE Hollow core doors are inexpensive and easy to customize. For this project, we embellished a salvaged door with bold blue paint and extra large furniture tacks.

RIGHT The color of the bumper pool table's felt top was a perfect match for the room and a yard sale score for just $100.

$100

We added color to otherwise ordinary wood built-ins by wallpapering the door fronts!

LEFT The family's Carnival masks now have a place of honor displayed on the built-in desk.

A Final Thought

Let's face it: media rooms are not the easiest to decorate. There are screens, electronics, DVDs, and in this case, a boatload of VCR tapes to deal with. The challenge here was finding ways to downplay the presence of media while also celebrating it—as we did with the vintage TV we repurposed into a side table. It's one of my favorite projects in this book. In fact, I have been hunting for another so I can make one for myself! I also absolutely love how we turned a boring china cabinet into a Moroccan-inspired showstopper that has both great form and function, hiding all those tapes. Both pieces were probably headed to the dump before we rescued, recycled, and reinvented them. To think, no one wanted them—and look at them now!

chapter 8

A COOL & COZY KITCHEN

Just a year after moving in, the owner of this home was diagnosed with breast cancer. Needless to say, decorating was hardly a priority. Five years later, and now in remission, this wife and mother of two is now ready to create a kitchen that mirrors her incredible energy and zest for life. Just like all of the things she wants to conquer, her kitchen ideas here have her begging the question—how to fit it all in? In addition to an updated cooking and prep zone, she wants a bigger island, and since there's no separate dining room in the house, she'd love a table at which to host parties. After all, there is a lot to celebrate!

1

THE FAMILY NEEDS A BIGGER ISLAND AND DINING TABLE.

2

THE ROOM NEEDS TO BE A FORMAL DINING ROOM AND RELAXED KITCHEN.

3

THE HODGEPODGE OF FURNITURE HAS NO PERSONALITY.

The Plan

Whipping up a delicious mix

This kitchen/dining room is going to require some heavy lifting from the team. It has a decent flow and plenty of storage space; however, the cabinets are dated and tired-looking. We'll lacquer them in white and replace the countertops with butcher blocks. We'll also switch out the old backsplash with classic ceramic subway tiles. Throughout the space, we'll use Mom's favorite color combination—crisp and clean navy blue and white with pops of citrine yellow—to add even more sunshine to this already happy home.

On my to-do list:

- Paint the walls navy and add beadboard and a chair rail.

- Find a long farm-style table that is better suited for the dimensions of the room, and add more seating so this family can get the party started!

- Sand, prime, and paint the cabinets, replace hardware, and update the backsplash with white subway tile.

- Since they are into all things organic and natural, I want to add lots of green plants and herbs for cooking.

We'll update the countertops, cabinets, and appliances too!

The tiny round table isn't going to cut it in the new kitchen's dining area. We'll replace it with a long farm table. The yellow walls will go from maize to amazing navy blue!

INSPIRATIONS

RIGHT I found these vintage signs at the Antiques Garage made for "Burma-Shave" shaving cream in the 1950s. Though the wood and paint were worn, the splash of red and fun words made them, well, top banana!

– shopping list –

- Dining table—large enough for eight people

- A set of dining chairs

- Overhead light fixtures to hang above the island and dining table

- A chest or buffet—to serve food on and to add more storage

- New appliances and countertops

- Navy and white fabric; yellow accessories

The Hunt

Mom has been through a lot, so I want to buy pieces that will make her smile (and give her exactly the style room she's been dreaming of)!

A fresh coat of paint and new fabric on the seats will freshen up this dull set of dining chairs-bought for just $50 at Brimfield.

RIGHT Trolling a thrift store for dishware and accessories that would complement our crisp color palette.

BELOW The deals at Brimfield can be eye-popping!

The stenciling on this antique crate gives it an industrial vibe. I bought it for $36 at Brimfield to use as a side table.

DEAL OR DEAL BREAKER?

Be sure there are no hidden problems with your flea market finds. The following aren't definite deal breakers, but be aware—they may require some attention and additional costs.

Chairs with very loose arms

Case furniture with cracked or broken legs

Wood pieces whose veneer is pulling away

Lucite pieces with lots of scratches— you will always see them

Chipped or cracked pottery, unless you really like it. The integrity is compromised, and repairs are costly and cannot be guaranteed.

the big REVEAL

THIS KITCHEN/DINING AREA went from drab to fab in no time flat. The navy and white backdrop is crisp and classic, just like Mom wanted. For the kids who also inhabit this space, the bold shots of zingy yellow and fun accessories keep it whimsical. Every single thing we put into this space, from the green plants to the kitchen table to the vintage wooden toys, has a backstory and, more important, a new lease on life just like the woman who inspired it.

before

Now We're Cookin'

The dated kitchen gets a brand-new look without a gut renovation!

The kitchen had a great layout but dated finishes—but not anymore! We painted the cabinets white, replaced the brown backsplash with crisp white ceramic subway tile, and installed dark walnut butcher-block countertops. The new countertop is warm, modern, and food-prep friendly.

This dining area opens up to the kitchen, so we wanted the two rooms to flow together. We put beadboard on the bottom third of the walls to mirror the lower cabinets on the other side of the room. Now it feels like a stylish, unified space!

1940s painted wooden farm animals are playful art pieces that keep with the room's happy-go-lucky style.

The charming vintage sign brings in an unexpected punch of red.

$100

$20

Completely
stainproof!

before

ABOVE We upholstered the family's barstools with one of my favorites—plastic shower curtains!

BELOW It always gets worse before it gets better! The team takes a moment to plan the next move after we've completely disassembled the room.

"To ensure their longevity, be sure to regularly rub wood countertops with butcher-block oil."

—DAVID

RIGHT I thought Cija might hit me with one of the legs she's holding when she first saw the condition this table was in.

before

"If you're worried about wear and tear on a painted tabletop, cover it with a piece of glass to protect it."

—CIJA

ABOVE Give some zig to your zag. The graphic look of chevron stripes plays well with so many styles. To achieve a uniform pattern, Jen created a computer blueprint tailored to the tabletop's dimensions and mapped it out using blue painter's tape.

The Table Turnaround

I should have followed my own advice before I bought the antique table pictured on the opposite page. I was so taken by the price that I overlooked its obvious flaws. It was really wobbly (meaning the legs would need to be reinforced,) but even more difficult to fix—it was so low that any long legged diner would bump their knees. I assumed my amazing team could add blocks to the legs to give a few inches of height to the legs with no problem—but you know the old saying about assuming. Poor Cija had her work cut out for her trying to salvage this hunk o' junk, which ultimately didn't happen. It just goes to show, even a seasoned secondhand hunter like myself can pick a clunker every once in a while. In the end the team was able to save the tabletop, but the entire frame had to be scrapped and rebuilt from scratch. Sorry Cija!

BELOW Sam found these antique industrial-size whisks in the bottom of a box at Brimfield. We paid $70 for each one. The seller told us they came out of a cupcake factory. This time around, we'll recycle them into delicious hanging fixtures. To electrify them, Alex used basic hardware: a wire, a socket, and some chain.

$70

$150

Industrial whisks look sweet as lights!

before

Hot Seats

The homeowners had four sturdy chairs around their old round table, and we found a different but similar set of four more at an estate sale. To turn the two sets of four dining chairs into one unified set, we painted them all the same crisp white. We covered all the seats in the same shiny navy-blue vinyl—an amazingly durable material that is stainproof and great for high-traffic areas. When the chairs are arranged around the table as a group, you hardly notice that they're different!

$95

We dressed up an array of flea market flowerpots with silver spray paint.

before

These framed sea fans make great organic art!

$10

$20

$35

Head(board) of the Class

This sleepy-looking headboard—bought for just $20—is now the life of the party as a beautiful bench. We built a wood base and attached the headboard to the back, and then painted it the same glossy white used throughout the rest of the room. The old floral fabric was swapped out with a large-scale navy and white print. It is now a king-size victory and a beautiful example of what smart secondhand design is all about: the rewards that come with a little re-imagination.

A Final Thought

Since Mom had battled cancer, we wanted to make this kitchen perfect for her—but we also kept the kids in mind with every choice we made. I love the silly red sign and the childlike vintage wooden farm animals that reside on the mantelpiece. All the seating was covered in vinyl—one of my favorite tricks—so it can be cleaned with a swipe of soap and water. And the color—it doesn't get more fun than that sunny yellow! It's now a space that maximizes family time with very little fuss. The only thing that can't be wiped away in here are the memories being made every single day.

The 1940s ceramic bowl, a $3 Goodwill find, is great for guacamole—or green plants.

chapter 9

A STUNNING STUDIO

When I set out to find a small apartment to use as an office/writing studio and occasional weekend getaway for my family, my expectations might have been a bit unrealistic. I wanted a great location, charming architectural details, and of course, a major bargain. After nitpicking through countless open houses with the most patient real estate agent in the world, I realized that something would have to give or it wasn't going to happen. I zoned in on a small studio in a generic building—not at all what I had envisioned—but what it lacked in old world charm, it more than made up for with a terrific view, an open floorplan, and even a small balcony! In decorating speak, it had great bones—bare and boring, but they were there. Now we just needed to give it a little personality.

The Plan

Big ideas, small space

The 490-square-foot apartment is in good condition, but has zero personality and looks a bit tired. The kitchen counters and cabinets need updating; the wood floors need to be redone; the closet doors are flimsy and generic. The goal is to maximize the space so it's equally comfortable whether it's just me, or my husband and kids as well.

On my to-do list:

- Find furniture that can multitask—desks as dining tables, sofas as beds, and a coffee table with storage.

- Paint the floors a light color so the entire studio is one big, neutral backdrop for my quirky collection of furnishings.

- Update the kitchen cabinets and add a wood paneled wall to add warmth to the space.

- Use as many of my flea market finds as possible to clear out my storage unit, but exercise masterful restraint. In a small space, less is more!

before

The finish on the cabinets screams 1998!

before

It's not bad . . . just really boring. None of this is my style: the yellowish wood floor, the standard doorknobs, the brown granite countertops. Fortunately, though, it has a nice layout and great natural light.

INSPIRATIONS

BELOW A pair of '70s chrome and wicker armchairs are small enough to fit on the tiny balcony. All they need is new cushions and they'll be fab!

$55 at Brimfield!

ABOVE This vintage wooden screen from India, found at a New York City flea market for $200, will become the jumping-off point for the studio's style.

The Hunt

My flea market finds often lead me to a style for a room. In this case, I found myself gravitating toward industrial edginess and Indian-inspired patterns and designs.

BELOW Seaching for one-of-a-kind accessories at Elephant's Trunk Flea Market.

ABOVE LEFT The patina on this reclaimed wood table is great but it's too large for my tiny studio. I'll use it as inspiration.

ABOVE Nobody does the Indian-vibe thing better than designer John Robshaw. In his New York City showroom and on his website, there are hundreds of different patterns and colors to choose from!

— shopping list —

- Cool vintage art and maps
- Lighting
- Barstools
- A dramatic headboard
- Seating
- Bookcase or TV stand

ABOVE These ornate wood carved blocks are used to print fabric in India.

BELOW A vintage trunk like this will make the ideal coffee table. It's charming and gives me a place to stash stuff when I'm expecting company!

SECONDHAND STATS

Paris is home to the Marché aux Puces de Saint Ouen—Europe's largest flea market—which welcomes up to 180,000 visitors every weekend.

The doors get a coat of deep navy!

We prepped most of our projects in the "yard," my 24-square-foot balcony.

A quick sanding—a must before you paint floors.

Aaron rolls on gray paint.

On the Surface

How we got this studio to shine

I think it's pretty obvious by now: I'm obsessed with antiques and vintage pieces loaded with character. I never thought I would buy a cookie-cutter condo in the city, but when the price of this little guy dropped—then dropped again—I jumped on it. Sure, it was a great deal, but I knew from the get-go the team and I would have to put some serious elbow grease into making this studio apartment into a stunner.

The doors were basic and flimsy looking. We painted them a dark navy, but what really took them to the next level was the molding we tacked on to add some architectural interest. The finishing touch: replacing the lackluster doorknobs with a shiny chrome version we found online. New doors would have cost several hundred dollars. Our transformation only cost about $45 a door! (See them on page 175.)

A light gray painted floor makes the space look much bigger. Yes, it requires wipe-downs on a regular basis, but the visual is well worth the work. We used outdoor porch paint because it's very durable, even in high-traffic areas. The team recommends lightly sanding the floors, using an oil-based primer, and then at least two coats of paint. The floors will look slightly worn over time, but that's part of the appeal—they're not meant to be perfect. Invest in felt pads for any furniture pieces that might scratch the floor.

This gap has to go!

before

day 1

day 2

day 3

THE SIX-DAY KITCHEN MAKEOVER

DAY 1 The kitchen cabinets were super generic, super orange, and had a dust-collecting 7-inch gap above. I decided to remove the cabinet above the sink to create space for display shelves. I had the guys rip out the countertop and sink, but kept the cabinets and the appliances, which were in fine shape.

DAY 2 I found this super chic dimensional subway tile at my local home-improvement store. I've seen similar for three times the price in tile showrooms. The team installed them all the way to the ceiling to add vertical interest and used white grout to match the new snow-white quartz countertops.

DAY 3 These cabinets were anything but high end, but I knew running crown molding at the top would give them a custom-made look. We removed the doors and secured a long board above the cabinets to close off the gap. We also removed one cabinet so we could install open shelving.

DAY 4 We added small trim to conceal the gap between the old cabinet and the new board, as well as large crown molding.

DAY 5 The interior of each cabinet was taped off, and we lacquered everything in a color called Evening Note by Benjamin Moore. It's a rich shade of blue somewhere between royal and navy.

DAY 6 Alex and Aaron (an honorary design team member!) found old scaffold boards that made perfect chunky open shelves. They cut two to size and secured them to the surrounding cabinets.

day 1

day 5

day 6

the big
REVEAL

IT MAY NOT BE A LARGE SPACE, but it sure feels like it now! With almost every piece doing double duty, the 490-square-foot studio has separate areas to write, entertain, and relax in without feeling too busy or overstuffed. The space is now both, relaxing and inspiring. The blue and white palette used throughout keeps the open floor plan cohesive, and the Indian and industrial pieces add a hint of urban cool.

before

My office. Yes, it is actually a closet!

$120

We have a lot of rich fabrics in this room, so we kept the shape of the platform sofa really simple. Aaron built it in four pieces to fit in the narrow elevators and screwed it all together on-site.

Indian + Industrial = Inspiring!

Dreamy double-duty solutions

To create as much seating as possible, we designed a custom L-shaped platform sofa that easily becomes beds for each of my kids. Just toss the pillows in a closet, throw a sheet on there, and it's lights out. The platforms are made of plywood and topped with 6-inch down and foam cushions—firm enough to snooze on comfortably, but also cozy enough to snuggle on while watching TV.

Over in the sleeping alcove, the small closet was unusable once we installed the queen-size bed. Instead of forfeiting the storage though, we simply removed the door and turned it into a tiny but terrific office! We wallpapered the interior so it's glamorous and inviting, then found a pint-sized lamp to illuminate the space. A shelf was installed at desk height so I can sit and work at my computer, and the additional shelves house magazines and files.

An authentic Air France poster from the '20s found for $50 hangs over my bed!

$40

ABOVE The closet was partially blocked by the bed, so we removed the door to create the world's smallest office

LEFT Less is more when it comes to using a busy patterned wallpaper like this one by Cole and Sons.

LEFT Taking out one cabinet makes the kitchen look larger and creates a nice focal point from the living area.

BELOW The barstools with carved wooden seats look like they were custom made for this apartment. The metal hairpin legs add a mid-century touch.

RIGHT We had just enough laminate wood flooring from the wall project to cover the dated tile floor in the kitchen. The rustic look is a nice contrast to the glossy cabinets and white countertop.

The Floor/Wall Switcheroo

A home usually has painted walls and wood floors, right? but why not do the opposite? Using outdoor porch paint, the grey floors are now one shade darker than the wall color to give them the slightest bit of contrast. A real wood-paneled wall would cost a fortune, so we re-created the look using wood laminate flooring from a home-improvement store. The browns and grays warm up the room and accentuate the bar area.

We used store-bought flooring for the walls!

This "cow-bra" rug is a zebra pattern printed on a cow skin.

All the fabrics in the studio came from designer John Robshaw!

The screen is my headboard!

$200

$40

We mounted the bookcase on these old wheels I bought for $8!

Old Vs. New

I always prefer to decorate with cool vintage finds but there are always exceptions, like the bookcase I envisioned for the studio. I searched high and low for an industrial-style piece to house my TV, electronics and collection of art books, but it had to be extra-narrow so it didn't eat up any more space than absolutely necessary—after all, in a space this small, every inch counts. I also wanted it to be extra-tall for more storage, and to emphasize the high ceilings and add storage. In the end, this fantasy bookcase did not exist, so I had the team build one to my exact specifications.

ABOVE The Indian screen hangs above the bed to create a dramatic headboard. Placing the bed horizontally gives it the feeling of a casual daybed and takes less up less space.

BELOW This 1970s Lucite bar, found at a New York City flea market for just $120, is the perfect size and width for the nook in the entry hall. It serves as both a bar and a place to drop the keys and mail, and it even lights up!

I've been collecting '60s barware for years. Now I have a perfect spot to show it off.

$120

These chairs came from a Paris flea market!

"When having furniture custom made, always ask the maker to test the stain on a scrap. Every species of wood accepts stain differently."

—ALEX

Out of Sight

New York City apartments rarely have central air and heating. Instead, they have clunky old units that aren't exactly pretty and take up precious real estate. To hide mine and to add surface area for lamps and writing, the team built an industrial style console that slides right over it. When I have guests over, I turn these chairs around so they face the L-shaped sofa, creating a cozy conversation area.

This solid brass rhino is one of my favorite finds!

$35

$5

TOP RIGHT The accessories are a mix of new and old: one-of-a-kind treasures, containers, vases, and even a large brass rhino—captured on eBay for $35.

RIGHT A silver plate peacock tray is tarnished to perfection. It was found at a flea market for just $5!

"Wiring a chandelier into the ceiling costs a fortune.
Why not hang it from a chain? It's a bohemian look
and will only cost you $35 in supplies!"

—JEN

ABOVE This '60s Tole chandelier adds Asian flare above the bed. With no room for nightstands, it offers much needed light for nighttime reading.

FACING PAGE The chandelier's wire and chain are barely noticeable, tucked alongside the wooden screen.

$25

ABOVE The '70s rattan chairs, sprayed with a clear weather seal and re-covered in sunbrella fabric, make a cozy gathering spot on my tiny terrace.

A Final Thought

Who says bigger is better? My 490-square-foot studio feels like it's twice the size, thanks to streamlined furniture that does double-duty and a color palette that is clean and simple. We used every single square inch of the space to its maximum potential by turning one of the closets into a desk area and making the seating area work overtime as both a sofa and beds for the kids. I followed my mom's decorating mantra—less is more. The only art on the walls are the vintage maps, one large mirror, and a pair of small flea market paintings. Anything more would have made the small space look cluttered, and it's all that was needed to give the tiny space a big personality.

Love,
Lara

Out of the closet! Me, taking a little break from writing this book in my "office."

UPHOLSTERY GUIDE

You've seen the amazing deals we've found throughout the book, but don't forget to factor in the price of refurbishing your finds. Here, fabric guru Sam Knapp shares a basic guide to how much upholstery could cost. Prices will vary depending on where you live. Be sure to get more than one estimate.

SOFA

Yards needed: 18–30, depending on size and repeat of pattern
Cost: $950–$1,395

BERGÈRE CHAIR

Yards needed: 3
Cost: $550–$695

ARMCHAIR

Yards needed: 7–10
Cost: $550–$695

BENCH

Yards needed: 1–2½
Cost: $195–$350

LOVE SEAT

Yards needed: 10–15, depending on size and repeat of pattern
Cost: $750–$950

HEADBOARD

Yards needed: 2 for twin, 3 for full/queen, 3 for king
Cost: $395–$895

DINING CHAIR

Yards needed: 1
Cost: $75-295
Cost depends on whether the seat pops off or not. If so, try doing it yourself with a staple gun.

CHAISE

Yards needed: 8–15
Cost: $695–$895
Tufting and piping cost extra

CURTAINS

Yards needed: 3½–4 per panel and depends on ceiling height
Cost: $195–$1,395
Lining costs extra

REFINISHING GUIDE

Sometimes all a piece needs is a quick coat of spray paint. But if something requires repair, restoration, or a complete overhaul, leave it to the experts. Here, Mark Devito, our resident furniture expert, shares some of the most common finishing processes.

DINING TABLE

Cost: $750–$1,500
Cost will vary depending on whether the base is pedestal or legs.

ARMOIRE

Cost: $1,000–$1,500
Interior work is extra

BERGÈRE CHAIR

Cost: $250–$500

GLOSSARY

FRENCH POLISHING
The method of applying a finish with a wrapped cotton ball and cloth, dampened with a thin finish and streaked onto furniture.

LACQUERING
The process of using clear or colored coatings that results in a very hard, shiny, durable finish.

LEMON OIL
An oil commonly used in furniture repair that cleans, shines, and moisturizes wood.

REFINISHING
Stripping an existing finish off and applying a new one.

RESTORATION
Adding a finish on top of an existing finish.

STRIPPING
The removal of the existing finish completely down to the wood.

TOUCH-UP
To clean, fill scratches, touch up color where needed, wax, or rub with lemon oil.

DINING CHAIR

Cost: $150–$300
Armchairs are
$50–$100 extra

CREDENZA/DRESSER

Cost: $700–$1,200
Interior work is extra

COFFEE TABLE

Cost: $300–$600

FLEA MARKET FABULOUS RESOURCES

AARON KEITH DESIGNS
A talented custom furniture builder that created some of the pieces in my studio

Based out of New York, New York
aaronmadeit.com

THE ANTIQUES GARAGE
A fabulous flea market tucked into a multilevel garage space in Hell's Kitchen

112 West 25th Street
New York, New York 10001
212-243-5343
hellskitchenfleamarket.com

BLACK ROCK GALLERIES
A giant emporium of used and vintage pieces ranging from high-end to diamonds in the rough

1720 Fairfield Avenue
Bridgeport, Connecticut 06605
203-335-0000
blackrockgalleries.com

BRIMFIELD ANTIQUE SHOW AND FLEA MARKET
One of the largest and oldest outdoor flea markets in the United States—a must-visit!

23 Main Street (Town Hall)
Brimfield, Massachusetts 01010
413-245-0030
brimfield.com

BROOKLYN FLEA MARKET
Brooklyn's finest! An indoor/outdoor flea market featuring vintage wares (and great food) in New York City's coolest borough

Multiple locations in Brooklyn, New York
brooklynflea.com

BUILD IT GREEN! NYC
A New York City nonprofit that sells salvaged and surplus building materials

Multiple locations in Brooklyn and Queens, New York
bignyc.org

CLARKE BUILDERS
David Dall's family business. They design and build custom homes in Connecticut

PO Box 187
Riverside, Connecticut 06878
203-637-4135
clarkebuilders.com

CONSIGN IT GREENWICH, INC.
An always-packed consignment shop run by estate-sale gurus

115 Mason Street
Greenwich, Connecticut 06830
203-869-9836
consignitgreenwich.com

ELEPHANT'S TRUNK FLEA MARKET
It doesn't get more charming or authentic than this outdoor flea in the Connecticut countryside

490 Danbury Road
New Milford, Connecticut 06776
860-355-1448
etflea.com

GOOD GOODS
Beautiful upholstery fabrics and designer drapery (and some discontinued finds!) at great prices

859 Boston Post Road
Darien, Connecticut 06820
203-655-8100

GREENFLEA MARKET
The Upper West Side's most outstanding indoor/outdoor flea market

100 West 77th Street (School)
Columbus Avenue between West 76th and 77th Streets
New York, New York 10024
212-239-3025
greenfleamarkets.com

HOUSING WORKS THRIFT STORES
Benefits those living with AIDS

Multiple locations in New York
housingworks.org

JEN CHU DESIGN
My awesome project manager, Jen is also an interior designer and decorator

Based out of New York, New York
jenchudesign.com

JOHN ROBSHAW TEXTILES
Luxurious block-printed textiles inspired by India

245 West 29th Street, Suite 1501
New York, New York 10001
212-594-6006
johnrobshaw.com

JONATHAN ADLER
Modern, happy, and chic furniture and accessories by the iconic designer, potter, and author

Multiple locations nationwide
jonathanadler.com

LENNY'S CUSTOM DECORATING SERVICES
Lenny has upholstered dozens of pieces for me over the years

141 Main Street, 2nd Floor
Norwalk, Connecticut 06851
203-807-8462

RAPHAEL'S FURNITURE RESTORATION
Mark Devito's is a true magician—he can bring any antique piece back to its former glory!

652 Glenbrook Road, Unit #9-101
Stamford, Connecticut 06906
203-348-3079
raphaelsfurniture.com

RESTORATION HARDWARE
Timeless, classic-looking home furnishings and decor (I especially love their lighting)

Multiple locations nationwide
restorationhardware.com

ROSE BOWL FLEA MARKET
One of my favorite flea markets in California!

1001 Rose Bowl Drive
Pasadena, California 91103
323-560-7469
rosebowlstadium.com

TIGER LILY'S GREENWICH
Samantha Knapp's family store features custom upholstery, pillows, and accessories

154 Prospect Street
Greenwich, Connecticut 06830
203-629-6510
tigerlilysgreenwich.com

For more resources nationwide and in-depth information about secondhand shopping, see my book *I Brake for Yard Sales.*

Acknowledgments

My eternal gratitude goes out to the folks that helped me bring this book to life. It was not exactly the best timing, trying to write it while shooting not one but two shows for HGTV during the summer of 2014, but Sue Seide and Terri Murray from HGTV helped me find the 25th hour in each day. Your patience, ideas, and chardonnay (when needed) will never be forgotten.

The hands-on talent I got to witness while creating the rooms in this book was simply incredible. This team, whom I am honored to work with each season on *Flea Market Flip*, can perform miracles—and on a couple of occasions, they were asked to do just that. Thank you Jen Chu, Mark Devito, Alex Guerrero, Cija Johnson, David Dall, Sam Knapp, and the rest of the gang for making some of the longest days also the most fun.

Thank you, ChiChi Ubiña, for catching every detail in your pictures, and thanks to Scripps and HGTV for the terrific shot on the cover.

A giant thank-you to my writer and part-time therapist Amy Feezor, who helped me organize and write every single page of this book—and who even stayed focused on it while visiting Paris! J'adore!

I am forever grateful to my *GMA* family, starting with Kelly and Sabrina. The Greenwich Bureau is a 24/7 operation and knows no bounds when it comes to getting the job done. You make me feel safe and loved, and for that, I will forever be loyal.

To my bosses—Tom Cibrowski, James Goldston, Ben Sherwood, Barbara Fedida—thank you for your un-wavering support and friendship. I am so lucky to be able to share my passion for hunting and decorating with our viewers. I get to go yard saling and it's actually considered work! How great is that?

To Robin, George, Amy, and Ginger—thank you for being such great teammates. I know you don't always understand my exuberance over the junk I find but you always play along! I love you guys.

Robin, Kathy Griffin, and Rachael Ray—I am honored to have your kind words grace the cover of this book, and honored to be your friend.

I want to thank the team from Abrams Books—Dervla Kelly, Rebecca Kaplan, and Michael Jacobs—and my agents, Andy McNichol and Jon Rosen, for making this happen.

A major shout out to my mom—who taught me how to spot a diamond in the rough—my dad up in heaven, and my four brothers and sisters, who keep me humble and laughing always.

Mad love and thanks to my husband and best friend, David, for helping me create the two greatest treasures on the planet, Duff and Kate.

And finally, to my kids, Duff and Kate—thank you for letting me take over your section of the garage for all my projects and finds. I love you both so much and promise to stop redecorating your rooms. (For now.)

XOXO,

LARA

Published in 2014 by Stewart, Tabori & Chang
An imprint of ABRAMS

Text copyright © 2014 Lara Spencer and Amy Feezor
Photographs copyright © 2014 ChiChi Ubiña, UV Studios

Additional photography credits:
Page 6, copyright © 2014 Sabrina Peduto
Page 7, copyright © 2014 Jonathan Adler Studio
Pages 10 (top and bottom left), 20 (bottom), 25 (bottom), 26 (top), 41 (bottom right), 48 (middle left), 60 (top and middle), 61 (bottom), 74, 78 (bottom left), 92 (top), 100 (bottom), 137 (bottom right), 162, 165 (top and middle right), 166, 167, 168 (left), 170 (middle and bottom left), 171 (top and bottom left), 177 (top and bottom), 179 (top left), copyright © 2014 Jen Chu
Pages 11 (top), 13 (top and bottom left), 18, 22 (left), 38 (left), 45 (top), 51 (middle right), 58 (right), 76 (left), 78 (top right), 79, 84 (top left), 88 (middle and bottom left), 89 (top right), 100 (top left), 101 (top right), 104 (bottom left), 110 (top left), 116, 124 (bottom), 133 (bottom left), 150 (left), 164 (top right), copyright © 2014 Christine Lockerby
Pages 11 (bottom right), 14 (middle right), 15 (middle right), 83, 89 (bottom right), 95 (bottom), 127 (bottom), 143 (middle and bottom right), 153 (bottom), copyright ©2014 HGTV/Scripps Networks, LLC. / Leon Barber
Pages 13 (bottom right), 14 (top and bottom right), 15 (top right and bottom), 46 (top right), 55 (bottom right), 67 (bottom), 68 (bottom right), 73 (bottom right), 104 (top and bottom right), 105 (bottom left and middle), 109 (top right), 111 (bottom right), 113 (bottom), 142 (top and middle left), 152, 156 (top left), 158 (bottom right), copyright ©2014 HGTV/Scripps Networks, LLC. / Ryan Scott
Pages 24 (bottom), 30 (top right), copyright ©2014 HGTV/Scripps Networks, LLC. / Joseph Pickard
Pages 29 (top and bottom right), 78 (bottom right), 80 (bottom), 81 (top right), 148 (middle left), 149 (top left), 165 (bottom), copyright ©2014 HGTV/Scripps Networks, LLC. / Tina Rupp
Pages 118 (left), 123 (bottom left), copyright © 2014 Despina Alexiou

Library on Congress Control Number: 2013945640
ISBN: 978-1-61769-095-2

Editor: Dervla Kelly
Designer: Jen Chu
Production Manager: Tina Cameron

The text of this book was composed in Garamond Premier Pro, Brandon Grotesque, Pistilli, and Rockwell

Printed and bound in the United States of America

10 9 8 7 6 5 4 3 2

Stewart, Tabori & Chang books are available at special discounts when purchased in quantity for premiums and promotions as well as fundraising or educational use. Special editions can also be created to specification. For details, contact specialsales@abramsbooks.com or the address below

ABRAMS
THE ART OF BOOKS SINCE 1949
115 West 18th Street
New York, NY 10011
www.abramsbooks.com